"Penny Cooke's work takes the reader to the heart of God the Father and draws them closer to His expressed wish that we *talk with Him* . . . that we bring the little things as well as the big things into His throne room . . . that we leave the heart of who we are with the heart of who He is. She reminds us that God waits for His children, desiring them to lean in, lean on, and trust fully that He is big enough to meet all our needs. These conversations are not only for the trials of life but for the everyday."

—Eva Marie Everson,
best-selling author and president of Word Weavers International

"If you're looking for a more meaningful prayer life and deeper communication with Papa God, I highly recommend *Pursuing PRAYER*. Author Penny Cooke, in her reader-friendly, let's-get-real conversational style, uses relevant Scripture alongside marvelous quotes from contemporary faith giants to renew your passion for truly effective prayer. Whether you do the study on your own or in a group setting, it'll be six weeks of investment in your faith walk that you'll always cherish."

—Debora M. Coty,
speaker and award-winning author of more than forty inspirational
books, including the best-selling Too Blessed to Be Stressed series

"*Wow!* I've read most everything I can get my hands on regarding prayer, and this is one of the simplest, warmest, and most inviting books I've ever read. How could it not be? Penny is a simple, warm, and inviting person. When I met Penny, she was leading a weekend retreat, and I was her speaker. I knew right away we were going to have a great weekend because that retreat had been prayed over. I don't think it would have mattered if I'd sang 'The Star Spangled Banner' . . . the Holy Spirit was going to work because Penny's team had been praying! And that is exactly what happened. How exciting it is to read her book. I hear her voice and see her smile. With encouragement and 'come alongside-ness' Penny guides you through a step-by-step understanding of how to begin the adventure of prayer. While the mystery of prayer continues to baffle most of us—Penny draws you into this wonderful relationship, and you come out the winner. You will enjoy this study—whether you participate in it alone or with a group."

—Leighann McCoy,
author of *Spiritual Warfare for Women* and
founder of The Prayer Clinic Ministry

"Penny Cooke has unlocked a key to making our prayers touch eternity. Using her Bible study and PRAYER acrostic can turn your prayer time into a power that will not only change your life but will also breach the very walls of God's throne. She embraces the might of Jesus' blood and applies logic to give even someone new to prayer a means to embrace God's communication conduit—prayer."

—Jill Bond,
author of *Dinner's in the Freezer, Writing to God's Glory,*
and others, and publisher of *Blessed Living Women's E-Magazine*

"Penny Cooke provides each believer the discipline of discovering the life God meant for each one of us. *Pursuing PRAYER* demonstrates how we can come to know God's good, acceptable, and perfect will for our lives. This is a study into the heart of God and His desire to have a close and personal relationship with His children through prayer."

—Gary Townsend,
North Florida Regional Catalyst, Florida Baptist Convention

"Penny's book is a joy to read because I know Penny's story, and I know she really prays! In *Pursuing PRAYER*, you'll be motivated to want to pray, equipped in how to pray, challenged to commit to pray, and inspired by Penny's own life and practice of prayer to fervently and faithfully pray as you trust in God and await His answers. Saturated in Scripture and rich in practical application, *Pursuing PRAYER* will challenge you to connect and commune with God in a way that might just be life-changing for you—and for those for whom you pray."

—Dr. Paul A. Thompson,
senior pastor of Calvary Baptist Church, Dothan, AL

Pursuing Prayer

BEING EFFECTIVE IN A BUSY WORLD

PENNY COOKE

NEW HOPE®
PUBLISHERS
Imprint of Iron Stream Media

Birmingham, AL

New Hope Publishers
An imprint of Iron Stream Media
100 Missionary Drive
Birmingham, AL 35242
NewHopePublishers.com

Library of Congress Cataloging-in-Publication Data

Names: Cooke, Penny, 1954- author.
Title: Pursuing prayer : being effective in a busy world / Penny Cooke.
Description: First edition. | Birmingham : New Hope Publishers, 2019.
Identifiers: LCCN 2019022490 (print) | LCCN 2019022491 (ebook) | ISBN 9781563092879 (trade paperback) | ISBN 9781563092886 (epub)
Subjects: LCSH: Prayer—Christianity—Textbooks.
Classification: LCC BV215 .C68 2019 (print) | LCC BV215 (ebook) | DDC 248.3/2--dc23
LC record available at https://lccn.loc.gov/2019022490
LC ebook record available at https://lccn.loc.gov/2019022491

ISBN-13: 978-1-56309-287-9
Ebook ISBN: 978-1-56309-288-6

1 2 3 4 5—23 22 21 20 19

This book is dedicated to:

My mother Alice, who taught me by example to read
my Bible each day. Her consistent devotional time was
inspiring and one to follow.

And to her sister, "Ant" Peggy, who taught me the Lord's Prayer
during a visit from out of state when I was a little girl,
complete with "I love you, Jesus" at the end.

These two women faced many trials, but I am deeply grateful
for their strong faith and unswerving examples.

Contents

Thank you!

A special thank you to my writer friend, mentor, and teacher, Jill Bond, for her constant encouragement and cheerleading, as well as proofreading and fact checking.

And thank you to those who did this study as a test run and encouraged me. My love and appreciation to you all.

Introduction

Thank you for choosing this book and desiring to have a more meaningful, effective prayer life. God desires that for you too, which is why you have this book in front of you right now. I believe it is not by chance. Whether you have chosen to do this in your daily quiet time or as a group study, God is drawing you closer to Himself to do a mighty work through you through prayer. I'm so glad you've responded.

We will discuss the elements of prayer Jesus taught in the Lord's Prayer and why they are vital to one's prayer life today. Before we get into the meat of the study, we will assess our prayer life in order to see how we can improve.

More than a how-to or book of prayers, this is a practical book meant to stir inspiration and motivation to pursue prayer proactively, regularly, and fervently. People can be taught what prayer is and how to pray, but it is up to them to do it. This book will motivate you to prayer by increasing your faith and your desire to pray. It will help those who struggle to implement prayer in their busy, overbooked schedules and will ignite a renewed passion for prayer. Please understand, this is not a set of rules to follow but rather a quest to see how we can be more effective in our praying in a mixed-up world that desperately needs our prayers.

If you have participated in other Bible studies, you may find this one a bit different, as you will have four days of lessons each week instead of the typical five. I have found many Bible study attendees end up rushing to get the fifth day done because they spend weekends with their family and one day is their Bible study group day, so they actually only have four days to complete the lessons. In addition, when going over the lessons, groups often do not have time for the fifth day. Therefore, the fifth day in this study is a review day, because that's what we do in our groups—review the lessons. I highly recommend individuals, as well as group studiers, to complete the designated review for the fifth day. This will help solidify what you've studied throughout the four days. For those who would like a full fifth day, there is an additional exercises each week for further study, which can be done any time during the week.

You will find instructions for groups and individuals on Day Five of each week's lessons. The questions designated with a heart (♥) are the suggested questions to go over together with your group or to review as an individual. Of course leaders are welcome to choose other questions they think their group would like to discuss.

Group time can be structured as follows:

- Open in prayer. (Instruction for the Introductory Group Session is at the beginning of Week One, and all other group session instructions are on Day Five.)
- Review lessons from Day One through Day Four.
- Take group prayer requests (space provided at the end of each group session).
- Close in prayer.

Note: How much time you allow for review will depend on how much time you have for your group. I suggest determining a certain amount of time for each day's review to keep things flowing and assure you get through all four days.

During your personal study, remember to begin each day with prayer, asking God to speak to you, open your heart to what He has to teach you, and help you apply what you have read.

I'm praying for each person who reads this book to be motivated to have deeper, more productive prayers and for your new fervent, effective prayer life to avail much (James 5:16 NKJV)!

Blessings!

WELCOME

Welcome to the *Pursuing PRAYER* Bible study! This study is about being proactive and intentional about prayer. We will use an acrostic for prayer, and each week we will use a different letter of the acrostic to study a different aspect of prayer based on the Lord's Prayer in Matthew 6, as well as many other Scripture passages.

You may use this book in your personal devotional time or as a group study. (If you're doing this study as an individual, consider asking a friend to join you so you can discuss it each week.)

The daily readings will take about twenty minutes to complete, and each week includes an optional exercise for further study. You may want to plan ahead for this week's optional section, which is found after Day Four but can be done any time during your week.

We will go deeper into actual Bible study in the following weeks, but the first week we are setting the stage, so to speak. As we begin our journey, we are going to spend a little time assessing our own prayer life.

Note: No one should feel bad or guilty if you're not where you think you should be in your prayer life. This assessment is intended to show us personally where we can improve, and we all can. The questions that follow are for your benefit alone, so answer them honestly. But if you choose to share your personal answers in a group, can we all agree that what is said in our group stays in our group?

Great! Let's dive in!

Date I began this study: _____

INTRODUCTORY SESSION LEADER GUIDE FOR GROUPS

Welcome and get to know the members of your group. Provide books if members do not already have one. Pray to open.

Read the Welcome from page xiii together.

Ask:

What is prayer?

What has been your prayer experience thus far? Do you have struggles or frustrations with prayer?

If you were to teach someone to pray, what would you tell them, and how would you instruct them?

Ask if anyone would like to share an answered prayer.

Note: You will have four days of lessons each week and an additional optional exercise for further study. The fifth day is a review for individuals or a time for groups to review their answers together. (If you have to miss your group time, you may do the review for individuals for that week.) Please make every effort to finish this book to get the most out of it. If one day doesn't particularly peek your interest, don't give up. The next day may be just what you need to hear.

Please do your best to finish your lessons each week, but don't let an unfinished lesson keep you from attending your group time. We all understand life happens. Come and be part of your group so you can benefit from that portion of the study.

Watch Video P. Discuss what impacted you the most and why.

Before closing, take time for prayer. When taking prayer requests, suggest to your group to be sensitive of others' time. Resist asking questions about a person's request until after so everyone will have a chance to share. After the prayer time, you may discuss the details, if desired. You can write your group's requests down on the Group Prayer Request section provided each week. This will help you remember to pray for your group members when you begin your lesson and will serve as a reminder to follow up later.

WEEK ONE

Pursue Prayer Proactively

Theme: Proactively pursue the privilege of prayer in order to prevail.

Day One

PURSUE PRAYER
PROACTIVELY

Pray then like this.

—Matthew 6:9

All Christians pray.

Or do they?

In my experience in women's ministry and life coaching, I've talked with many women who say they struggle in this area. They say they don't pray enough or haven't really prayed about that yet or don't have time. Studies on prayer reveal similar findings (see Week Two, Day One). I've even known some who profess to have a special prayer language but say they hardly ever use it.

When I was in third grade I was given a Bible by the church my family attended. I don't remember being told to read it, although I'm sure I was, but I do remember seeing my mother read hers, and so I began to read mine. I grew up reading that little black Bible nearly every night before I went to sleep.

I read the Book of Psalms a lot, so much so that to this day I can still recite a few of them (such as Psalm 121) from memory.

I lift up my eyes to the hills. From where does my help come? My help comes from the LORD, who made heaven and earth. He will not let your foot be moved; he who keeps you will not slumber. Behold, he who keeps Israel will neither slumber nor sleep. The

LORD is your keeper; the LORD is your shade on your right hand. The sun shall not strike you by day, nor the moon by night. The LORD will keep you from all evil; he will keep your life. The LORD will keep your going out and your coming in from this time forth and forevermore.

—Psalm 121

The Psalms are prayers in song. They developed my faith and taught me to pray. They taught me of a faithful God in whom I could pour out my heart and place my trust. Psalms taught me life is not always easy, but God is always there to help, guide, and comfort.

Perhaps that's why I have such a passion for prayer today. Oh yes, I struggle sometimes, like everyone else. But throughout my life I have found God to be faithful in many hard situations, just as He was for the psalmists. Thus the reason for this book. This study provides the opportunity to develop and increase that same kind of reliance on our faithful God.

No matter where you are in your prayer life—whether you are a seasoned pray-er, someone struggling to believe prayer works, or frustrated trying to find the time—this study is for you.

I'm so glad you've joined me.

As we begin, jot down what you'd like to get out of this study.

♥ Record your initial thoughts. Why pray?

When was the last time you prayed?

How often do you pray more than a popcorn prayer?

Do you have any doubts as to whether your prayers work? (It's okay. You can be honest.)

Record what insights the following verses give as to some reasons we should pray. (I promise you won't always have this many verses to look up, but for now, it's important as we begin our study.) I've started you off with the first two.

Psalm 23:4   When in fear; when in need of comfort.

Psalm 31:3   For guidance.

Psalm 32:5

Psalm 46:1

Psalm 95:6

Psalm 118:19

Matthew 26:41

John 15:7

James 1:5

James 5:16

♥ Which one or two of these verses speaks to you the most and why?

The first reason to pray is simply because we as believers are instructed to (Matthew 26:41; Luke 18:1; Ephesians 6:18–19; Philippians 4:6; 1 Thessalonians 5:17; 1 Timothy 2:1).

> **To be a Christian without prayer is no more possible than to be alive without breathing.**
>
> **—Martin Luther**

In *Tyranny of the Urgent*, Charles E. Hummel says, "The root of all sin is self-sufficiency—independence from the rule of God." To *not* pray is to say we do not need Him. He quotes P. T. Forsyth, who says, "The worst sin is prayerlessness."

♥ Did you ever think of not praying as sin?

Look with me at James 4:17, and fill in the blanks to complete. (The primary Scripture translation I use throughout is the English Standard Version, and I will let you know if I use any other translation.)

So whoever knows the _____ thing to do and _____ to do it, for him it is _____.

> Far be it from me that I should sin against the LORD by ceasing to pray for you.
>
> —1 Samuel 12:23

Sin isn't just doing something we're not supposed to do. It can be *not* doing something we *are* supposed to do. This is often called the sin of omission. No worries, friends. Do not be discouraged. God will forgive you. When we study the Bible, we realize all the people God used, even in the lineage of Jesus, were flawed just like us.

It's remarkable to look at David, for instance. He was a liar, adulterer, even a murderer, and yet God graciously called him a man after God's own heart.

Wow! That means there's hope for us. Even the most faithful of God's people weren't faithful all the time. As a matter of fact, we all can be like yo-yos. We spin downward, and God has to continually wind us back to Him. Oh, the amazement of God's grace . . . but that's for another day. Let's get back to the subject of prayer.

Considering we don't always do what we should, an important part of prayer is confession. Take a look at James 5:16. What is the first thing James tells us to do?

Confession is what makes a righteous person (not good deeds), and righteousness is what makes our prayers powerful and effective.

♥ Take a moment to see how David talked to God about this in Psalm 51:1–12 and 17. Record your thoughts.

We'll talk more about confession and forgiveness later in this study, but I wanted to touch on it here because today's intention is for us to understand the seriousness of prayer, not to feel bad if we haven't been praying enough. God has plenty of grace for that. Let's close today with 1 John 1:9 in mind, "If we confess our sin, he is faithful and just to forgive us our sins and to cleanse from all unrighteousness."

What is your main takeaway from today's beginning lesson?

Day one—done! Thanks for being here. I look forward to our time together tomorrow.

Day Two

PURSUE PRAYER'S PURPOSE, PARTNERSHIP, AND POWER

Let us then with confidence draw near to the throne
of grace, that we may receive mercy and find grace
to help in time of need.

—Hebrews 4:16

A friend of mine recently shared she was journaling and speaking to God about the longing she had for a moment of her husband's undivided attention. She wanted him to want to spend more time with her, to focus on and nurture their relationship in the same way he did his business. She soon heard the Lord speak to her heart, "Child, don't you realize that's what I want from you, a moment of your undivided attention? You're so distracted trying to fix things on your own. I want you to seek Me and My kingdom, and you will have everything you need."

Yesterday we looked at many reasons to pray. Let's look at a few more today.

Prayer's Purpose

One of the most important purposes of prayer is relationship. We are not only instructed to pray, we are *invited* into His presence (Isaiah 55:1–3; Jeremiah 33:3; Matthew 11:28; Luke 11:9–10; Philippians 4:6; Hebrews 4:16; Revelation 22:17).

Prayer is a privileged invitation from a Holy God (who is also called *Abba*, an Aramaic word meaning Daddy, in Mark 14:36; Romans 8:15; and Galatians 4:6). We get to crawl up in His lap and talk to Him. How awesome

is that? He wants to have a relationship with us. As a result, He meets
our spiritual and emotional needs.
Isn't that precisely what we're all
looking for? We often look for people and things to meet those needs,
but we were made to need Him. He
is our Creator and the greatest satis-
faction for our longing souls. He fills
the God-shaped hole in all our hearts.

> **Oh, what peace we often forfeit,**
> **Oh, what needless pain we bear,**
> **All because we do not carry,**
> **Everything to God in prayer!**
>
> **—Joseph M. Scriven,**
> **"What A Friend We Have in Jesus"**

What would our relationship be with our friends, children, or spouse if
we hardly ever spent quality time with them? Some may argue they have
quality time even if not quantity, but often quantity *is* quality when it comes
to time with the Lord.

God promised if we seek Him first, He will take care of the rest.

> Seek first his kingdom and his righteousness, and all these things
> will be given to you as well.
>
> —Matthew 6:33 NIV

♥ According to Matthew 6:33, what are we to seek?

When are we to seek it?

What will be given to us if we do?

What are "these things?" (See verses 31 and 32.)

There you have it. We need not worry. Everything we *need* is found in Him. And yet so often, we go to Him last.

After a particularly moving church service, people often like to say, "God showed up."

God did not "show up." God was already there. We show up. When we accept His invitation to meet with Him in worship or in prayer, we sense His presence, and amazing things happen.

My friend essentially wanted her husband to show up emotionally. But she realized if she would consistently seek God first, she would not be looking to her husband to fill all her emotional needs, which no man can do and many a man has been frustrated trying to fulfill. She discovered God is very present, even when her husband isn't. She now basks in God's undivided attention. She realizes He longs to nurture their relationship, as well as her relationship with her husband. And He has.

Prayer's Partnership

A partnership is a relationship involving equal rights and responsibilities. Partners have the same interests and priorities. In a game, partners play together against an opposing side.

In prayer, we partner with God. We share the right to His presence and a responsibility to His will. We even partner together against an opposing side. So another purpose of prayer is to partner with Him by asking Him to do what He already wills to do. Prayer moves the hand of God.

That's why Jesus told the disciples in Matthew 6:8, "Your Father knows what you need before you ask him."

Prayer brings about the will and power of God.

Prayer also brings our desires in line with His will and desires. Jesus modeled this when He, about to face the most horrific death, prayed to His Father, "Not my will, but yours, be done" (Luke 22:42).

♥ If something is His will, why do you think we have to pray for Him to do it?

Partnering with God in prayer is joining Him in His will. It's agreeing with Him and working with Him. He gives us free will, so it's up to us to choose to partner with Him or not.

But you know what they say—be careful what you pray for. On the continuum below, mark honestly whether you think you really want God's will in your life.

|---|

No, thank you.   Yes, please.

Share about a time you offered help or advice to a friend or loved one who didn't want it.

Share about a time when you were too prideful to take someone's help or advice.

God knows this about us. He knows we're not prone to take advice unless we ask.

He wants us to ask. And when we do? Prayer releases God's power to accomplish His perfect will. In this way, we partner with Him. We partner with Him when we join Him in His will. We partner with Him when we are willing to let Him use us to accomplish His will. How gracious He is to allow us to play a part and involve us in His sovereign process.

Prayer's Power

Prayer is one of the pieces of the spiritual armor we are commanded to put on. Ephesians 6 speaks of taking the sword of the Spirit, which is the Word of God, and praying at all times.

The Message paraphrases Ephesians 6:13–18 this way:

Be prepared. You're up against far more than you can handle on your own. Take all the help you can get, every weapon God has issued, so that when it's all over but the shouting you'll still be on your feet. Truth, righteousness, peace, faith, and salvation are more than words. Learn how to apply them. You'll need them throughout your life. God's Word is an indispensable weapon. In the same way, prayer is essential in this ongoing warfare. Pray hard and long. Pray for your brothers and sisters. Keep your eyes open. Keep each other's spirits up so that no one falls behind or drops out.

In her *Daniel* Bible study, Beth Moore suggests we have no idea what unseen activity surrounds us. She imagines Christ saying to us one day, "Take a look at this scene with me, Child. I want you to see what was going on in the heavens when you were going through that crisis. Look at all that happened in your behalf. Gaze at that great cloud of witnesses cheering you on to victory." And this happens because of prayer.

Why do you think God doesn't always answer the first time? Why does it sometimes take so long?

Ultimately we are in a spiritual battle. Some battles are bigger and take more time. They cause us to have to fight harder and longer. This is one reason 1 Thessalonians 5:17 tells us to pray without ceasing and Jesus told the disciples in Luke 18:1 to always pray and not lose heart. We'll talk more about that in Week Six.

♥ If you have asked Jesus Christ to be your Lord and Savior, what does Ephesians 3:20 and Romans 8:11 tell us is inside every believer?

The Holy Spirit allows us to be continually in His presence. To pray without ceasing is a mindfulness of His constant presence, His unceasing readiness to listen, and His unlimited power to help at all times. We are to be as unceasing in our readiness to pray. We are to be proactive in our prayers.

This is why we are told in Ephesians 6:18–19 to pray at all times (*The Message*: "hard and long") and not cease (*The Message*: "falls behind or drops out") or, as Luke 18:1 puts it, "lose heart."

Is there anything you lost heart praying for because it didn't happen soon enough?

Although God's power is always available, when we neglect or cease to pray in any way for any period of time, we interrupt the flow of His power working in our lives and the situations we face.

> Indeed nothing will avail without prayer. Pray, whether you can or not. . . . You will surely find an answer of peace.
>
> —John Wesley

♥ What does the last part of James 4:2 say is the reason we do not have those things we desire?

♥ And yet what did Jesus say in John 14:13–14?

♥ In light of the previous verses, why would we not ask and keep asking?

Think of your favorite lamp. As pretty and able to cast light as it may be, it's useless unless you turn it on. But the power is still there. Think of prayer as accessing God's power.

> For we do not wrestle against flesh and blood, but against the rulers, against the authorities, against the cosmic powers over this present darkness, against the spiritual forces of evil in the heavenly places. Therefore, take up the whole armor of God . . . praying at all times.
>
> —Ephesians 6:12–13, 18

The armor of God consists of truth, righteousness, peace, faith, salvation, and the Word of God—six pieces. And then the Apostle Paul wraps it all up by saying, "praying at all times," as though prayer is the superglue that holds all the other pieces on.

In the Bible, the number seven represents completion. I see prayer as the seventh piece that completes the armor.

When we neglect to wear this vital piece of the armor, we allow the enemy to advance against us. We in a sense raise a white flag of busyness, carelessness, and apathy, resulting in defeat. Prayer is a powerful weapon in a life filled with spiritual warfare.

Trends show that women are becoming more and more passionate about social justice issues, but our society will not be changed apart from the prevailing power of proactive, persistent prayer. Our passion for prayer must be first.

Jesus said we would have tribulation in the world (John 16:33). So let's access His power—let's put our armor on, stand up (or shall I say, kneel down), and fight in prayer.

Do you possess the Holy Spirit? Second Corinthians 13:5 says, "Examine yourselves, to see whether you are in the faith. Test yourselves. Or do you not realize this about yourselves, that Jesus Christ is in you?—unless indeed you fail to meet the test!"

One of the purposes of this study is to assess your prayer life. In doing so, you must examine your spiritual life in general. Have you been a casual Christian, going through the motions? Have you been a backsliding Christian? Do you need to recommit your life to Christ in order to press the reset button on your prayer life and see God working powerfully through your prayers?

Perhaps you've never actually committed your life to Christ. Have you asked Jesus Christ to cleanse you of your sins and be your Lord and Savior?

Whether this is all new to you or you have attended church all your life, Jesus wants a personal relationship with you, not just for you to be part of a church or religion. This relationship begins when you ask Him to forgive your sins. No one and no church can do this for you. It is a decision you must make in faith. Romans 10:9–10 says:

> If you confess with your mouth that Jesus is Lord and believe in your heart that God raised him from the dead, you will be saved. For with the heart one believes and is justified, and with the mouth one confesses and is saved.

It is also not our good deeds that will allow us into heaven one day. The Bible says everyone has sinned (Romans 3:23), and it is our faith and His grace that will save us, not our works (Ephesians 2:8–9). Titus 3:4–6 says:

> But when the goodness and loving kindness of God our Savior appeared, he saved us, not because of works done by us in righteousness, but according to his own mercy, by the washing of regeneration and renewal of the Holy Spirit, whom he poured out on us richly through Jesus Christ our Savior.

When you confess your sins and ask Jesus to be Lord of your life, His Holy Spirit comes to live inside your heart to help you live the Christian life.

> Repent and be baptized every one of you in the name of Jesus Christ for the forgiveness of your sins, and you will receive the gift of the Holy Spirit.
>
> —Acts 2:38

> But to all who did receive him, who believed in his name, he gave the right to become children of God, who were born, not of blood nor of the will of the flesh nor of the will of man, but of God.
>
> —John 1:12–13

You may pray something like this: *Dear Heavenly Father, I know You are the Creator and Savior of humankind. I realize I have sinned against You, and I need Your forgiveness. I believe You died for my sins, and I accept Your forgiveness provided for me on the Cross. Please come into my heart and life. I receive Your Spirit, and I choose to follow You. Thank You for Your love and grace. In Jesus' name, amen.*

Please note, it's not necessarily a prayer like this that saves you. As stated in Romans 10:10, it's a heart issue. When I began my journey with Christ, I hadn't said a prayer, but I began to believe in my heart and to confess Him with my mouth, and soon I knew I was born again. A prayer like the one above simply helps you put what's in your heart into words.

> Therefore, if anyone is in Christ, he is a new creation. The old has passed away; behold, the new has come.
>
> —2 Corinthians 5:17

If you prayed that prayer, contact your pastor, a local church leader, or a trusted Christian friend or family member. They would love to know about it, pray for you, and answer any questions you may have. I would also love to know about your decision. You may contact me via my website at pennycookeauthor.com.

Day Three

PURSUE PRAYER ON
PURPOSE WITH PURPOSE

For this reason I bow my knees before the father . . . to be strengthened with power through his Spirit in your inner being.

—Ephesians 3:14–15

Have you struggled with neglecting prayer, finding it hard to set aside time? If so, you are certainly not alone. I too, and many others I've talked with, have struggled with this vital part of Christian living as busyness takes over so often. But I've also known intimacy with God in prayer and the peace and joy (and answers) that come through intentional, persistent times of heartfelt prayer. I long for that to be the norm for all of us so our lives and our world will be transformed.

Let's answer the following questions to further assess our prayer lives. (Note: If you are doing this study with a group, this assessment is solely for your own benefit and will not be shared in your group.)

Corrie Ten Boom once asked, "Is prayer your steering wheel or your spare tire?" Has prayer mostly been your steering wheel or your spare tire?

How would you describe most of your prayers?

___ What prayers?

___ Short and sassy (I'm really busy.)

___ Medium and mundane (Yawn)

___ Medium but meaningful (We talk often.)

___ Long and lofty (I've got this down.)

When was the last time you sat down and poured your heart out to God—and let Him pour His heart into you?

How did you feel after praying this way?

How often do you pray this way?

What keeps you from praying like this more often?

♥ When do you find it hardest to pray? Easiest?

Which one of the times you mentioned in the previous question do you think you need to pray the most?

Which do you do more of? Circle one:

Read Devotionals   Read Your Bible   Pray   None

Check all the reasons you have not been praying more:

___ I don't know how or where to start.

___ It's hard to sit still. I can't quiet my mind and am too distracted.

___ It's hard to surrender. I want to be in control, and I'm afraid to let God take charge.

___ Life is hectic. I'm up and going in the morning and nodding off at night.

___ I've gotten out of the habit. I just don't even think to pray until a crisis arises.

___ I don't see the necessity, and I don't really think He'll answer me anyway.

___ I don't want to bother God. He's got bigger prayers to answer.

___ I've been away from Him too long.

___ I'm not good enough for God to answer me.

___ I'm angry with God for not answering in the past.

___ Actually, I'm doing great in this area.

___ Other: _____

Tough questions, I know. But please do not feel bad; we all falter in our spiritual journeys. Remember, this is to help us all assess how we're doing so we can do better. I hope you've gained insight into your own prayer life so far.

Prayer is vital. But many of us don't pray enough, and in some cases, hardly at all.

One reason we don't pray enough is we, especially as nurturing women, are so busy tending to everyone else's needs, we often neglect ourselves, and our Lord, in the process.

We wouldn't go without eating for long periods of time or we'd become malnourished, yet we allow ourselves to be spiritually malnourished. We wouldn't think of not charging our cell phones (some of us even have back-up chargers), yet too often we go about our days spiritually uncharged. And forbid that we should miss answering a text right away, sometimes even while driving!

Are we too busy? If so, how can we *not* pray about all we have going on?

♥ Describe what it would look like if we treated our prayer life as diligently as we treat our cell phones.

♥ Read Proverbs 31:10–31 and Luke 10:38–42. Who do you relate to more and why? Circle one:

The Proverbs 31 Woman   Martha   Mary

Do you see more value in being the Proverbs 31 Woman or Martha than you do Mary sitting at the feet of Jesus? Why or why not?

What does the amount of time you spend in prayer and reading your Bible say about which one of these women you really value most?

Read Ephesians 3:14–19. What does Paul say he's praying for in verses 16 and 19?

How are you currently becoming strengthened in your "inner being" and "filled with all the fullness of God"?

Being filled with the fullness of God happens by purposely sitting at the feet of Jesus, praying and reading His Word. Men often think their most important responsibility is to provide for their family. Women are nurturers and tend to think it's virtuous to care for themselves last. Both neglect the inner being. In reality, we are not helping our loved ones by neglecting our inner self. For what do we have to pour out if we have nothing to fill ourselves up with? It is more beneficial to serve out of an overflow than the scrap at the bottom.

It would be helpful for us to remember the airplane principle—to put the oxygen mask on yourself before others—spiritually speaking, that is. What a wonderful example we could set for our children. Will they grow up remembering us reading our Bible and praying? Or will they grow up repeating our frenzy, without their spiritual armor?

> **In our rushing, bulls in china shops, we break our own lives.**
>
> **—Ann Voskamp,**
> ***One Thousand Gifts***

Which scenario do you exemplify?

Which do you *want* to exemplify?

What steps can you take to improve your prayer life?

What small step can you begin with?

♥ What does Ephesians 3:20 say God is able to do for us?

♥ Why, then, do you think so many people are not asking?

As I pondered this subject of prayer and prayerlessness, I sensed the Lord telling me that we, the church, are like Jesus' disciples who slept when He asked them to pray (Matthew 26:36–46). He needed them to take Him seriously and pray for what was about to take place, but they kept falling asleep.

> Fervent (*energeo*) means to be engaged in; to be active; to put forth power; to be at work, like an electrical current energizing the light bulb in the lamp we talked about yesterday. It is where we get our word *energy*.

Aren't we the same? Our families, our nation, and our world are spinning out of control. Yet many are not praying, and many others pray inconsistently, casually, and vaguely. Why? Because we are busy, distracted, and careless. Today's disciples have theoretically fallen asleep.

♥ Let's remind ourselves of what James 4:2b tells us.

♥ What does James 5:16b say prayer will do?

♥ What kind of prayer has great power?

♥ The King James Version uses the word *fervent* in James 5:16b. According to the definition of *fervent* above, describe what fervent prayer is.

How often do you pray these kinds of prayers? What are they usually for?

♥ The King James Version also uses the word *much* in the same verse. What do you think *much* means?

What "much" do you think you could have missed because you did not ask?

♥ What "much" might the church, our country, and world be lacking because Christians have become too busy to pray for them?

Imagine how many prayers go unanswered because they were not prayed. Imagine the good things that may not have happened because we did not pray them into existence. Imagine the peace, strength, comfort, wisdom, and direction we might have missed because we neglected to pray. Prayer is *that* vital.

> O Jerusalem, I have posted watchmen on your walls; they will pray day and night, continually. Take no rest, all you who pray to the Lord. Give the Lord no rest until he completes his work, until he makes Jerusalem the pride of the earth.
>
> —Isaiah 62:6–7 NLT

Let's purposely pursue God in prayer until we prevail. Let's pray fervently and continually, giving ourselves and Him no rest until we see our prayers established.

If you could go back and do it over, what would you pray for now that you neglected in the past?

> In Colossians 4:12, always *struggling* (*agonizomai*) on your behalf in his prayers (*laboring fervently* KJV), literally means to strive, contend, or fight as in an intense athletic contest or warfare. It's where we get our word *agonize*. It means to be utterly stretched to the max. I picture a worn-out runner crossing the finish line with his arms stretched out. Jesus certainly demonstrated this kind of fervency for us on the Cross. His arms continue to be stretched out for us today, eagerly welcoming us into fervent prayer.

What is something you'd like to see happen but haven't really prayed about yet? What if you stopped and prayed fervently for it right now? (Go ahead. I'll wait.)

If you have been negligent in your prayer life, ask God to forgive you for taking the privilege of prayer lightly. Remember what 1 John 1:9 says, "If we confess our sins, he is faithful and just to forgive us our sins and to cleanse us from all unrighteousness." Thank Him for His grace, and ask Him to use this study to help you grow in this area. He wants to meet you in prayer and is waiting for you to sit at His feet so He can pour His love and blessings on you. What power we miss when we miss prayer time with our all-powerful God!

Thanks for participating in these tough couple of days with me. I promise tomorrow won't be so heavy. I'm looking forward to it.

> Let us therefore come boldly to the throne of grace, that we may obtain mercy and find grace to help in time of need.
>
> —Hebrews 4:16 NKJV

Day Four

PLAN TO ENTER HIS PRESENCE AND DO NOT PROCRASTINATE

> You will seek me and find me, when you seek me with
> all your heart.
>
> —Jeremiah 29:13

Eleanor Roosevelt once said, "It takes as much energy to wish as it does to plan." I would add, it takes even more energy to regret what we planned but never did. Today's study is about planning. But to the point, a plan without action is only a wish.

Part of assessing our prayer life is taking some actions to help us be more intentional about prayer. And any successful action begins with a clear plan.

Plan Your Prayer Time

This study is about being more proactive about our prayer life. If you haven't already done so, pick a specific time that is best for you to have regular prayer time, a time that is more intimate, fervent, and effective.

Circle the best description of your prayer life.

Daily in my quiet time   Daily on the go   Occasionally   911!   Hardly ever

♥ What did Jesus do in Mark 1:35, and why do you think He did this?

Why is Jesus' example important for you and me?

Wouldn't you agree time alone with a spouse or friend is much richer than when people are around, and deeper meaningful conversations are more fulfilling than short (no matter how sweet) exchanges? It is the same with God. Jesus was intentional about prayer. He set an example of having a quiet time, or devotional time. He modeled being alone with God for a meaningful period of time, not just quickly or on the go. But in our busy lives, we must be proactive about it.

> **God designed the human machine to run on Himself. He Himself is the fuel our spirits were designed to burn.**
>
> —C. S. Lewis, *Mere Christianity*

♥ According to Jeremiah 29:13 how should we seek God?

> **Earnest: an intense state of mind; gravely important; serious. To seek God earnestly is to seek Him "with all our heart."**

Psalm 63:1 (NIV) says, "Earnestly I seek you." The King James Version says *early* instead of *earnestly.* (I guess you have to be earnest to be early.) The word translated earnestly is *shachar,* which literally means to look for early and diligently.

♥ Why do you think it's important to seek Him "early"?

Perhaps *early* can mean different things to different people. Some interpret it as "early in the day," and Jesus certainly exemplified that. We can't ignore the benefit of going to Him before the concerns of our day begin. But perhaps for you, early in the afternoon or evening would be the most opportune time. We can also seek Him early in a situation instead of waiting until it has become a crisis. We can seek Him before an event or activity. The point is to seek Him earnestly, not always quickly or only on the go. Certainly, late is never the best time.

When is your early?

Remember, we have an enemy who does not *want* us to pray. Therefore, whenever your early is, determine to be proactive about it, and plan by choosing a specific time to pray that works for your schedule. Being earnest means being committed to it in spite of all that will come against it. There will be days we just don't feel like it, and we have to make ourselves do it. We must not procrastinate. This is the time to remember it is a matter of obedience to His commands and not circumstances or feelings.

Procrastinate: to not be earnest; to not be early; to lack diligence

After examining your schedule, what can you rearrange or give up in order to be more earnest in your prayer time?

Read Psalm 42:2. When can *you* go meet with God?

What specific time and how much time will you commit to your proactive, planned time with God?

Prepare a Private Place for Prayer

Not only did Jesus pray early, He often purposely went to secluded places to be alone with God. Though we can pray anywhere, it is helpful to have a personal place for earnest, fervent prayer. I don't know about you, but I have different rooms in my house for specific things. It just works best that way. I wouldn't want the toilet in the kitchen or the stove in the bedroom. I used to drag my sewing machine out into the kitchen, which was inconvenient and made me lack incentive to sew. But now I have a specific sewing spot in the laundry room, and I am so much more motivated.

♥ Where do we see Jesus going in the following verses?

Luke 5:16

Luke 6:12

Luke 9:28

Jesus proactively pursued prayer by making a point to be alone to pray, and I'm pretty sure He planned it that way. The Son of God had no place to lay His head (Matthew 8:20), so He didn't have His own home where He could set a place aside. His place had to be different all the time. But we can have our own private place for regular, intentional, planned prayer time that is free of distractions. (Be sure to see the addendum, Six Tips for Distracted Prayer.)

Just as having a planned time to pray is beneficial, your special place should be conveniently equipped with your Bible, a pen, and paper or a journal.

Take some time to prepare your special place to pray, if you do not already have one. Perhaps you have a place, but it's not equipped with items that make it convenient. I recommend having a Bible you can keep there, if possible, not one you may risk leaving at church or in your car. A study Bible is best. You may want to have other items available also, such as a Bible dictionary, concordance, or commentary (the Internet is useful, but if it's a distraction to be online, I suggest a good old-fashioned book) and a journal, a couple pens (I like to use mechanical pencils so I can erase and not have to sharpen), and a few highlighters. Set it up with a chair, table, and lamp if necessary and maybe a candle and vase of flowers to make it appealing. Your special place might be in a certain room, by your favorite window, in your yard or porch, or even a closet. Make it a place away from distractions, one where you look forward to being, and one that every time you see it you're reminded to pray.

♥ What do you think having a special place to pray communicates to those around you?

♥ What effect do you think this special place will have on you?

Of course we all have days we'll miss, but being proactive about prayer means protecting our prayer time as much as possible. Let your family or roommates know that this is your prayer place and your prayer time and to please try not to interrupt unless it is absolutely necessary (unless, of course, they'd like to join you). It may take a while, but if you are committed (earnest) and you don't give in to minor interruptions, they will catch on. And they just might catch *it*.

You've done great assessing your prayer life this week. For some it wasn't easy, but your new commitment will be so worth it. I can't wait to get into the heart of the study with you next week.

In closing let's read and meditate on Psalm 43:3–4, and record your thoughts.

♥ Share with your group about your special prayer place. Did you have any difficulties or distractions trying to create or maintain your prayer place? Do you have any helpful suggestions for others in your group?

I bow my knees before the Father . . . that according to the riches of his glory he may grant you to be strengthened with power through his Spirit in your inner being, so that Christ may dwell in your hearts through faith . . . that you may be filled with all the fullness of God.

—Ephesians 3:14–19

You finished the first four days. Great start!

For Further Study

PRAY DAY

[Jesus] said to Peter, "So, could you not watch
with me one hour?"

—Matthew 26:40

*L*et's practice being proactive about prayer by spending some time in your special prayer place reading Scripture, worshipping, praying, and journaling. You may want to plan for this in advance so you can spend at least an hour, hopefully more, maybe even a whole morning or a whole day.

Some of you do this often; for some this will be a new activity. For others, especially those with little ones or fulltime jobs as well as a family life, getting an hour to yourself is a rarity. I understand, but do the best you can. No matter your situation or how long you choose, it is sure to be a blessing.

For many, it will simply be a discipline to make yourself sit still that long with a Bible in hand instead of a phone. I know it can be hard, but as Psalm 46:10 says, we must be still (cease, be idle) to know (be aware, perceive) that He is God (supreme, mighty).

If you're new to Bible reading, the Book of Psalms is a great place to camp out and pray. I suggest starting with Psalms 19; 103; or 145. Perhaps you can find some of your own favorites. If you listen to Christian music, play some of your favorites and have a time of worship. Pray and ask the Lord to reveal to you what He wants to say to you through what you read.

And as Hannah, who prayed so fervently she was mistaken for being drunk and replied, "I have been pouring out my soul before the LORD"

(1 Samuel 1:15), pour out your own soul before the God who longs to spend time with you.

Record your experience.

> There are times when solitude is better than society, and silence is wiser than speech. We should be better Christians if we were more alone, waiting upon God, and gathering through meditation on His Word spiritual strength for labor in His service. We ought to muse upon the things of God, because we thus get the real nutriment out of them. . . .
>
> Why is it that some Christians, although they hear many sermons, make but slow advances in the divine life? Because they neglect their closets, and do not thoughtfully meditate on God's Word. They love the wheat, but they do not grind it; they would have the corn, but they will not go forth into the fields to gather it; the fruit hangs upon the tree, but they will not pluck it; the water flows at their feet, but they will not stoop to drink it. From such folly deliver us, Oh Lord.
> —Charles Spurgeon, *The Devotional Classics of C. H. Spurgeon*

♥ Is there anything about this time you would like to briefly share with your group?

Day Five

WEEK IN REVIEW

I will lift up my eyes to the hills—from whence comes my help?
My help comes from the LORD, who made heaven and earth.

—Psalm 121:1–2 NKJV

Pursue Prayer Proactively

Pursue Prayer's Purpose, Partnership, and Power

Pursue Prayer on Purpose with Purpose

Plan to Enter His Presence and Do Not Procrastinate

<u>For All Participants</u>:
Contemplate—How has your view of prayer changed as a result of this week's study?

Consider—What one thing do you want to remember most from this week's study?

Commit—What change will you make or action will you take as a result of this week's study?

For Individuals:
Go back through the week's sessions and reread anything you may have highlighted, and review the questions designated with the heart (♥). If you have not done the exercise for further study from this week, consider doing it today.

Session One Leader Guide for Groups:
Welcome attendees back. Pray to open.
Ask: How has your view of prayer changed as a result of this week's study?

Go over the questions from Week One designated with a heart (♥), as well as the contemplate-consider-commit questions, if there is time.

Ask if anyone would like to share about her optional prayer experience.

Watch Video R1 and discuss.

Take prayer requests (please keep them short so everyone can share), and close in prayer.

WEEK TWO

Remember His Righteous Deeds

Theme: We must remember who
God is and what He has done—both in the Bible
and for us personally—before we can truly "hallow His name."

Day One

REMEMBER HIS RIGHTEOUS DEEDS

Hallowed be thy name.

—Matthew 6:9 KJV

Welcome back. This week our focus will be on the R of our acrostic, which stands for *remember*. We simply cannot hallow His name if we don't take time to remember what He has done for us, because remembering produces thankfulness, and thankfulness produces worship.

I'll be the first to admit I have a terrible memory. I find myself too often saying, "I can't remember what I was about to say," or "Did I already tell you this?" And why is it I can remember I put something in a special place, but I can't remember what the special place is? Furthermore, don't bother to call me on a Monday morning because I will likely miss your call, as my phone is sure to still be on silent from church on Sunday. How about you? How is your memory?

Let's begin our study today by reading 1 Chronicles 16:7–12 and answering a few questions.

When was thanksgiving to be given to the Lord (v. 7)?

List all the things they were to do (vv. 8–12):

♥ According to Psalm 100:4, how are we to enter His presence?

♥According to Philippians 4:6, what is to accompany our prayers?

To hallow—to set apart as holy

No wonder Jesus started the Lord's Prayer with "hallowed be thy name." Many of us pass right by this important aspect of prayer as we rattle off our lists and rote prayers. More than teaching a recited prayer, Jesus instructed His followers in the elements of prayer to be included, and worship was the first one.

What percentage of time do you give your prayers for worship, and what percentage do you give for personal requests?

According to LifeWay Research, 82 percent of praying people pray for family and friends and 74 percent for their own problems and difficulties. Only 12 percent pray for government leaders. Only 25 percent believe all their prayers are answered.

According to The Barna Group research, less than one out of every five Christians (18 percent) claims they are committed to investing in their own spiritual development. Less than one out of ten have had an *extended time of spiritual reflection during the past week*.

According to the Pew Research Center, only about half of Christians rely on prayer when making decisions. Women are more likely than men to pray every day, and older adults pray more than younger adults.

Thanksgiving is a natural part of worship. We cannot worship if we are not first thankful, and we cannot thank Him for what we do not *remember*.

In his book *Crazy Love*, pastor, speaker, and author Francis Chan states, "There is an epidemic of spiritual amnesia going around." What do you think he means, and do you agree with him?

Using more than one of our senses enhances learning and therefore memory. This is why journaling is so important and beneficial. Journaling helps us remember. Not only can we look back and *be* reminded, but writing things down also increases our memory.

> **One generation shall commend your works to another, and shall declare your mighty acts.**
> **—Psalm 145:4**

Journaling also helps keep us focused and our mind from wondering while we're praying. If you don't already journal, it's a great way to keep a record of your insights and prayers, including those little prayers God answers along the way that we may not notice or may easily forget. This can be so encouraging.

A journal can also be a sort of memorial. Memorials are important to God. We see them all through the Bible as sacrifices, stones, names, etc.

What important memorial is seen in Luke 22:17–20?

Read Joshua 4:1–7 and see what God commanded as a memorial, where it was taken from, and why.

♥ We keep all kinds of memorials, such as pictures or souvenirs. What else might you have in your home as a memorial?

♥ Can you think of a way to make a memorial to the Lord for something He has done in your life?

As we saw in Joshua, creating memorials can be a great way to teach children about the Lord.

In Exodus 3:15 God told Moses to tell the people the Lord sent him to them—what else did He tell him?

♥ Why is it so important to remember? What happens when we forget?

Read Judges 8:33–35 and summarize what it says.

The Bible tells us to remember and reminds us to not forget. In the following two verses, circle the things we are not to forget and underline the reasons why.

> Only take care, and keep your soul diligently, lest you forget the things that your eyes have seen, and lest they depart from your heart all the days of your life. Make them known to your children and your children's children.
>
> —Deuteronomy 4:9

> Do not forget my teaching, but let your heart keep my commands, for length of days and years of life and peace they will add to you.
>
> —Proverbs 3:1–2

Deuteronomy 6:12 instructs, "Take care lest you forget the LORD, who brought you out of the land of Egypt, out of the house of slavery." Is there some Egypt (bondage—habit, dependency, etc.) you need Him to set you free from? (Remember, He came to set you free. See Luke 4:18.)

What Egypt *has* He freed you from?

Have you returned to any Egypt in your life?

Have you wished you had not left some Egypt in your life or desired someone else's Egypt? (For example: the what ifs, if onlys, and the dreaded "coveting" the world dangles in our face as being better than what we presently have.)

So how can we say, as in the Lord's prayer, "Hallowed be thy name," if we are not mindful of what He has done for us or are desiring something other than what He's provided for us? How can we properly worship?

♥ Here is one especially for us women. What does Jeremiah 2:32 imply women remember, and what does it say they forget, and for how long?

Do you think this Scripture verse describes God's people today? How does your schedule and priorities show this to be true/not true in your life?

> **Remembering produces thankfulness, and thankfulness produces worship.**

Take some time today to remember, and list as many things as you can that God has done for you. Ask Him to bring things to mind. You may even include things He's forgiven you for. Once you've made your list, remember to thank Him for all He's done.

Remember the former things of old; for I am God, and there is no other; I am God, and there is none like me.

—Isaiah 46:9

Don't forget to return tomorrow.

Day Two

REMEMBER TO RETURN
TO HIM

And return to the LORD your God, you and your children, and
obey his voice in all that I command you today, with all your
heart and with all your soul.

—Deuteronomy 30:2

As we read yesterday, God repeatedly told His people *remember*.
Have we forgotten as the Israelites had? Could this be one
reason why many of today's believers have become lax about
praying?

The Old Testament is filled with stories of Israel's inconsistencies. I
can almost imagine God watching from His throne as He picked petals
off daisies. "They love Me, they love Me not, they love Me, they love
Me not . . ."

We don't have time to study all those Old Testament stories here, but
Psalm 106 recounts Israel's continual forgetfulness and rebellion paralleled
with God's continued mercy and grace. Let's read this Psalm and list in two
separate columns as many things as we can find they did or did not do
and what God did for them. (I'll give you extra space, but don't get bogged
down. If it takes too long, you can always finish later. Please don't skip this
exercise. It's important to see the faithfulness of God over and over through
this exercise.)

They Did/Did Not	**God Did**

♥ Circle one or two things that impress you the most in these lists.

I mentioned last week that we're all like spiritual yo-yos, but I think the Israelites invented the yo-yo. They were good for a while and God blessed them, then they became comfortable and forgot His blessings and provisions and backslid. They rebelled against Him, God warned them, they didn't listen, and God finally had no choice but to discipline them. They returned to Him, were good again, God blessed, and the process started all over again . . . up, down . . . up, down.

When I read through the Old Testament I think, *Wow, why didn't they remember and stay in line and avoid the consequences?* But, friends, *that's us too.* Whenever I hear "God's chosen people," I think, *Yeah, chosen as an example—an example of humankind.*

An example of me.

We too have turned our backs on God's principles and commands. Do you think we can expect the same discipline if we do not return? Many people see our problems as economic or political, but at the core we have a spiritual problem.

Second Chronicles 7:14 is an often-quoted verse. "If my people who are called by my name humble themselves, and pray and seek my face and turn from their wicked ways, then I will hear from heaven and will forgive their sin and heal their land."

Hmmm . . . If my people . . . pray . . . *then* I will heal.

Again, it all comes down to prayer. And remembering. And returning.

God's commands have not changed—He is the same yesterday, today, and forever (Hebrews 13:8). This is why we must pray consistently and fervently for our nation and return to *His* ways.

Take a look at Jeremiah 2:17 and 19. What brought on Israel's troubles?

♥ When does Deuteronomy 4:30 say the people will return to the Lord?

♥ In Jonah 2:7 when did Jonah remember and return to the Lord (or you could say, when did Jonah remember to pray)?

♥ Why do we so often wait until a crisis before we remember the Lord?

As a friend recently stated, "We don't get serious about prayer until things get serious." Sometimes life's seriousness is what makes us remember. But must God allow adverse circumstances to move us to seek Him?

God is the perfect parent. He does not go back on His word or forget to follow through with His warnings. He does not cave in or enable. He is our loving Father as well as our righteous Judge. Although He is patient, He will do what He says He will do. So when He warns, it is best we listen and heed because He *will* follow through in order to discipline us for our good. His purpose is to get us to return to His protection and loving care for our well-being (Proverbs 3:11–12).

No matter what, God's goal is always for our good and for restoration of our relationship with Him. He is our Heavenly Daddy and Shepherd, and He cares deeply for us and is always with us, ready to welcome us back no matter how far we stray. He calls to us in many ways, but sometimes He must use His shepherd's crook to drag us back. At times that's painful, but when He carries out this measure, it is always to prevent worse pain down the road.

You may have heard something like: "God doesn't cause things to happen, He *allows* them to." We could debate all day about such things. What matters is the lesson we learn from God's discipline and whether these times draw us closer to Him. And ultimately whether or not we return to Him. Because either way, that's the goal. So let's not get caught up in the hows and whys but more in the, "What is God saying to *me* personally through this? What am I learning, and how am I growing closer to Him as a result?"

What does Lamentations 3:40 say we must do?

♥ Read 2 Chronicles 30:9*b* and fill in the blanks:

The LORD your God is _____ and _____ and will not turn away his face from you, if you _____ to him.

Do you need to return to the Lord? Is there a part of your heart you need to give Him or return to Him?

Take some time to reflect and pray. Write down anything that comes to mind.

> But from there you will seek the LORD your God and you will find him, if you search after him with all your heart and with all your soul. When you are in tribulation, and all these things come upon you in the latter days, you will return to the LORD your God and obey his voice. For the LORD your God is a merciful God. He will not leave you or destroy you or forget the covenant with your fathers that He swore to them.
>
> —Deuteronomy 4:29–31

When we return, He redeems. See you tomorrow when you *return*.

Day Three

REMEMBER TO REJOICE

My soul will rejoice in the LORD and delight in his salvation.

—Psalm 35:9 NIV

When we *remember* what God has done and *return* to His ways, our natural response is to *rejoice*. This is when we can truly "hallow His name."

In the following verses, the Greek word translated "rejoice" (*agalliaó*) means to be exceedingly glad, to actually jump for joy.

Rejoice and be exceedingly glad, for great is your reward in heaven.

—Matthew 5:12 NKJV (emphasis added)

My spirit has *rejoiced* in God my Savior.

—Luke 1:47 NKJV (emphasis added)

In that hour Jesus *rejoiced* in the Spirit and said, "I thank You, Father."

—Luke 10:21 NKJV (emphasis added)

Have you ever been so excited you jumped for joy? Write about it.

♥ Have you ever been so thankful for something God has done that your *heart* jumped for joy?

I have. When my son married a wonderful Christian woman after being redeemed from a drug addiction, my heart jumped for joy. Each of my grandchildren have made my heart burst with joy as well. If you've reached *grand* status, I know you know what I'm talking about.

Still unborn, John the Baptist leaped for joy in his mother's womb in the presence of Jesus, who was in *His* mother's womb (Luke 1:41). Before anything happened on the outside, the Holy Spirit jumped for joy over the promised triumph!

Sometimes circumstances drown our joy, but when we rejoice in who God is and His promises, there can be joy amidst the pain, as we trust Him and He carries us through it.

> May my meditation be pleasing to him, for I rejoice in the LORD.
>
> —Psalm 104:34

In Psalm 104:34, *rejoice* is a little less "jumpy." Here the Hebrew word used (*samach*) means to be calmly happy, glad, or to cheer up. So to say *rejoice* here, you might say, "As I cheer up in the Lord."

Or in Philippians 4:4, which reads, "Rejoice in the Lord always; again I will say, rejoice." Here you could translate as, "Be *glad* in the Lord," "Be happy in the Lord," or "Cheer up in the Lord." I love this one—how do you cheer up when you're down? Cheer up in the Lord!

Fill in the blanks for Hebrews 13:15:

Through him then let us continually offer up a _____ _____ _____ to God, that is, the fruit of lips that _____ his name.

Why do you suppose the writer of Hebrews refers to prayers of thanksgiving as "sacrifices of praise"?

The word *sacrifice* here is written as a noun and refers to the actual sacrifice itself, the *thing* being sacrificed. The thing we sacrifice is our self. Our will. Our agenda. Our feelings. And we praise anyway. He is God and we are not.

So what is the difference between thanksgiving and rejoicing? Thanksgiving is a public acknowledgement or celebration of divine goodness. Rejoicing is to feel joy or great delight; exuberate; exult; triumph; glory. When we are obedient to being thankful, we will then feel like rejoicing.

It's easy to rejoice when things are going well. But praise and thanksgiving can be the last thing we think of when the medical report comes back positive, we have a prodigal child, or we suffer any pain or loss.

Those are the times when praise is a *sacrifice*. We die to self and put Him on the throne of our life even though we don't understand what is happening and why.

This is what it means to trust in the Lord with all your heart and not lean on your own understanding, to acknowledge (know, discover, understand for the sake of submission and thankfulness) Him in all your ways so He can make your paths straight (direct, make plain) (Proverbs 3:5–6).

These are the times we rejoice—"cheer up"—in the Lord.

♥ How often does Hebrews 13:15 say we are to offer a sacrifice of praise?

We are not to refrain under any circumstances—in good times *and* bad times.

♥ Look at Hebrews 13:15 again. With what are we to praise?

No matter what our hearts feel, we praise with our lips anyway. When obedient, feelings follow (this really works).

Have you ever praised God even though your heart was breaking? When?

What kinds of words are on your lips? Do you speak out of your *affliction* or out of your *affection for* God?

Our affection for God is why we are to make our requests with thanksgiving. We thank Him for what He is going to do as a result of our prayers; we thank Him for what He's done in the past; and we thank Him that He knows better what we need than we do.

So "cheer up!"

We cannot cheer up in the Lord apart from prayer and His Word. This is why it is essential to *remember to return* to Him each day.

♥ Describe Job, Nahum, and Habakkuk's attitudes in the following verses:

Job 13:15 and Job 19:25

Nahum 1:7

Habakkuk 3:17–19

♥ How does one cultivate such an attitude in the midst of loss and trials?

> When you wrap your prayers in awe and worship—concentrating on the *who* instead of the *whats, wheres, whys,* and *whens*—He rewards you with the knowledge that you are in the *presence of complete provision.*
>
> —Ken Hemphill, *The Prayer of Jesus* (emphasis added)

To rejoice in the midst of trials doesn't mean life won't hurt. It means you are not filled with anxiety (Philippians 4:6) because you're leaning on the only one who knows the end from the beginning (Psalm 139:16), who has the power to transform not only the situation but your heart (Romans 8:28; Ezekiel 36:26), and the one who can comfort your hurts like none other (2 Corinthians 1:3).

That's when His power is perfected (fully realized) in your weakness (2 Corinthians 12:9), and you experience peace that passes understanding (Philippians 4:7)—even though the storm still rages.

> But may all who seek you rejoice and be glad in you; may those who long for your saving help always say, "The LORD is great!"
>
> —Psalm 40:16 NIV

I'm rejoicing with you that you finished the first three days this week. And I'm praying you will discover His peace in your praises, no matter your circumstances.

Day Four

REMEMBER TO RAISE HIS NAMES IN PRAISE

For thus says the One who is high and lifted up, who inhabits eternity, whose name is Holy: "I dwell in the high and holy place."

—Isaiah 57:15

This week's focus has been worship, hallowing His name—making His name great. So today, we are going to do just that—Raise His names in praise! Let's take a long, hard look at Him through the following verses. Take time to meditate on each one, pondering what each says.

The LORD reigns; he is robed in majesty; the LORD is robed; he has put on strength as his belt. Yes, the world is established; it shall never be moved. Your throne is established from of old; you are from everlasting.

—Psalm 93:1–2

The LORD is high above all nations, and his glory above the heavens! Who is like the LORD our God, who is seated on high?

—Psalm 113:4–5

You have exalted above all things your name and your word.

—Psalm 138:2

Lift up your eyes on high and see: who created these? He who brings out their host by number, calling them all by name; by the greatness of his might and because he is strong in power, not one is missing.

—Isaiah 40:26

I am the LORD; that is my name; my glory I given to no other.

—Isaiah 42:8

♥ How do these verses speak to you? What stands out the most to you?

Let's not miss the fact that although He is our Creator, God Almighty, I AM, holy, awesome, and deserving of our reverence and worship, He is still personal. He abides with us, meets our needs and cares for us as His children.

> Only in the act of worship and praise can a person learn to believe in the goodness and greatness of God.
>
> —C. S. Lewis

Just listen to some of His personal names from Scripture:

Jehovah Ra'ah—The Lord Is My Shepherd (Psalm 23:1)

Jehovah Jireh—The Lord Who Provides (Genesis 22:14)

Jehovah Shalom—The Lord Is Peace (Judges 6:24)

El Roi—The God Who Sees (Genesis 16:13)

Jehovah Rapha—The Lord Who Heals (Exodus 15:26)

El Shaddai—The Almighty, All-Sufficient One (Genesis 17:1)

Jehovah Shammah—The Lord Is There (Ezekiel 48:35)

Hallowed be Thy names!

♥ When Abraham encountered God as *El Shaddai*, the all-sufficient God in Genesis 17:1–3, he could do nothing but fall face down before his

Almighty God. Another name for God is *El Elyon*, which means the God Most High. Yet where does God dwell and what does He do according to Isaiah 57:15?

Though Almighty God is Holy and dwells high above the heaven, He also chooses to dwell *in* us through the Holy Spirit. He revives those whose hearts are bowed down to Him.

> Therefore God has highly exalted him and bestowed on him the name that is above every name, so that at the name of Jesus every knee should bow, in heaven and on earth and under the earth, and every tongue confess that Jesus Christ is Lord, to the glory of God the Father.
>
> —Philippians 2:9–10

♥ What does 1 Corinthians 3:16 tells us we are?

♥ What does Colossians 1:27 call Christ dwelling in us?

Isn't it a comfort to worship a God we cannot exaggerate?

—Francis Chan, *Crazy Love*

Take heart. It *is* a great mystery, and we will never fully understand on this side of heaven. This high and holy God whose name is awesome chooses to dwell within us. If we understood it all, there would be no need for faith. Faith is belief in the unseen, and without faith it is impossible to please Him, because whoever would draw near to God must believe He exists and He rewards those who seek Him (see Hebrews 11:1 and 6).

♥ According to Psalm 113:2–3, when is the Lord's name to be blessed or praised?

Who is He to you, and what has He done for you? Look at the list of His names again. How has He been each one of those things to you? (If you're a new believer, look at His names and remind yourself that He *is* and will be all of those things for *you*.)

> "But what about you?" he asked. "Who do you say I am?"
>
> —Matthew 16:15 NIV

Why does God have so many names? Because one name could not describe His endless attributes, infinite sufficiency, and boundless power and glory. Make a list of as many one-word descriptions for Christ you can think of for what He has done for you personally (such

> **We've spent far too much time focusing on the mercy and grace of God and far too little time focusing on the glory of His name.**
>
> —**Leighann McCoy, *The Lord's Prayer***

as *Savior, comforter, guide*, etc.). Pray as you make your list, thanking Him for being each of those things to you, recalling specific circumstances. (Again, if you are a new believer, no worries if your list comes up short. It will grow over time.)

I call my list my memorial list, and I keep it in my Bible and add to it continually, using it often in the R (*remember/worship*) part of my prayer time. It has been such a blessing to me. I encourage you to do the same.

God has us on His memorial list too. Check out Psalm 139:16; Malachi 3:16; Philippians 4:3; and Revelation 3:5 and 21:27. When does Revelation 13:8 and 17:8 say God made His list?

What are your thoughts and feelings as you contemplate that God has had your name written in His book of life from the beginning of time?

> **When you hallow His name, you might just slip out of the Father's lap and onto the floor at His feet.**
>
> —Leighann McCoy, *Oh God, Please Teach Me to Pray*

I pray along with the psalmist that you may all rejoice and be glad in Him; that as you long for His saving help you will always say, "The LORD is great!" (Psalm 40:16 NIV).

We may forget to pick something up at the store, where we put our car keys, or what we went into that room for, but God's deeds, His commands, and His name are never to be forgotten.

And He will never forget you either (Isaiah 49:15)!

When you pray, don't forget to remember to rejoice and raise His names in praise.

You're doing great! I hope tomorrow's review will help you remember what we've discussed this week.

For Further Study

RECORD YOUR PRAISE

Write a prayer of praise to God here or in your journal. Do not rush through this. Dig deep. What does He mean to you? Use His names and the words you listed for Him from Day Four and the list you made on Day One of the things He has done for you. Pour your heart out to Him in worship. You may even want to spend some time listening to worship music.

Our Father which art in heaven, Hallowed be thy name.

—Matthew 6:9 KJV

Day Five

WEEK IN REVIEW

Enter his gates with thanksgiving, and his courts with praise!
Give thanks to him; bless his name!

—Psalm 100:4

Remember His Righteous Deeds

Remember to Return to Him

Remember to Rejoice

Remember to Raise His Names in Praise

For All Participants:
Contemplate—What are one or two things you want to remember most from this week's lessons?

Consider—What will you do to make sure you remember what you have learned?

Commit—What change will you make or action will you take as a result of this week's study?

<u>For Individuals</u>:
Go back through the week's sessions and reread anything you may have highlighted, and review the ♥ questions. If you have not done the activity for further study from this week, make a plan and schedule a time to do it.

<u>Session Two Leader Guide for Groups</u>:
Welcome attendees back. Pray to open.

Ask: What one or two things stood out to you the most this week?

Go over Week Two ♥ questions together, as well as the contemplate-consider-commit questions, if you have time.

If you are comfortable, share some of your words for God from Day Four.

Watch Video A and discuss.

Take prayer requests (remember to keep it short so everyone can share), and close in prayer.

WEEK THREE

Acknowledge Sin and Ask Forgiveness

**Theme: We receive His amazing grace
when we acknowledge sin
and adjust our life.**

Day One

ACKNOWLEDGE SIN AND ASK FORGIVENESS

If I had cherished sin in my heart, the Lord would
not have listened.

—Psalm 66:18 NIV

Welcome to Week Three of our study. Please don't skip out on me because I mentioned the word *sin*. This is not an easy topic, but hang in here with me through the week because this is an important issue, and I don't want you to miss God's freedom and grace.

This lesson conveys the *forgive us our debts* portion of the Lord's Prayer (Matthew 6:12). Last week we talked about worship. In remembering, we acknowledge who God is and worship Him appropriately. This week we acknowledge who *we* are in our sin and confess.

The godly acknowledge [sin] and seek reconciliation.

—Proverbs 14:9 NLT

Perhaps your Bible version uses the word *trespasses* for *sin*. Other versions may use *iniquity, transgression, wrongdoing,* or *offense*. No matter which word is used, sin is anything that breaks God's laws.

When we go against Him, we harm our relationship with Him, we harm ourselves, and we sometimes even harm those around us.

Sin is not a popular subject, even in some churches. We love to talk about God's grace, His mercy, and heaven, but we'd rather fluff over the subject of sin and hell. To complicate matters, the world tells us we must be *tolerant* and *politically correct* so as not to offend anyone by telling the truth about these realities (which is the most loving thing we can do). Proverbs 14:9 (NLT) says, "Fools make fun of guilt."

Any twelve-step program begins with the acknowledgement of a problem because one cannot address what one does not realize or will not admit. That's called denial. Denial is a slippery slope into an abyss of deep dark consequences. We must let Christ's love shine His light on our wrong and expose it for all it is—sin. But the gospel (literally, "good news") is that God has more than enough grace to cover all our sin, which we will discuss later in the week.

Sin is a difficult topic to write about. After all, who am I to talk about sin—I'm a sinner too (yet saved by grace, hallelujah!). But because of His mercy and grace, I ask you to allow me the "privilege of telling [you] about the endless treasures available to [you] in Christ" and that because of Him, "we can now come boldly and confidently into God's presence" (Ephesians 3:8 and 12 NLT).

It's crucial to come before our Holy God unencumbered by sin's blinders. Therefore sin must be dealt with for an effective prayer life, not to mention for our own peace of mind.

It is important to point out that we are not talking about the initial confession of sins for salvation (see Week One, Day Two) but rather the regular act of confession as a Christian.

Why do you think it is important to continue to confess even after salvation?

♥ Read James 5:16*a* and Galatians 6:1. What were Christians told to do in these verses?

The recipients of these letters were already Christians, saved by faith in Jesus Christ, but they were told to confess. So we know this isn't talking about initial salvation confession. Besides, faith is what gave them salvation (John 3:16; Acts 16:31; Romans 10:9–10), not their confession and repentance, which was a result of their belief. So in reality, even *that* confession was after salvation.

Upon salvation, our sinful nature is forgiven, but we still have it. Therefore we continue to do wrong things. We possess the Holy Spirit who helps us in our weakness (Romans 8:26), but we don't always rely on the Spirit's help, hence the need to continue to ask forgiveness as a believer.

Sometimes our human nature gets in the way, and we sin without meaning to. David asked forgiveness for "hidden faults" (Psalm 19:12). Can you think of hidden faults you may have?

Some things are hidden because we didn't mean to do them. But some are hidden intentionally by denying, ignoring, or rationalizing them. We earthlings don't admit failure easily, so it is wise to ask the Lord often to reveal anything in our life that offends Him.

Let's take a moment now to pray as David did in Psalm 139:23–24: "Search me, O God, and know my heart! Try me and know my thoughts! And see if there be any grievous way in me, and lead me in the way everlasting!"

Be still to hear God's still, small voice, and record what He brings to mind, asking for His sweet forgiveness.

Sin in the life of a believer is like fingerprints on glasses, which blurs you from clearly seeing Him working in your life. Or like a boulder on the road, tripping you and detouring you from the abundant life He has for you. Or it could be likened to an infection in your spiritual ear keeping you deaf to His still, small voice as He speaks to you. Confession is like the medicine that makes you well again, the eye glasses cleanser that helps you see clearly again, and the crane that comes and removes the boulder from your spiritual journey.

We must not only acknowledge we *are* sinners, we must acknowledge our *sins*. It is not enough to generally say each day, "Forgive my sins," we must say, "Forgive me for [fill in the blank]" and acknowledge specific sins, as it says in Leviticus 5:5 (NLT), "When you become aware of your guilt in any of these ways, you must confess your sin."

Okay, really, let's fill in the blank. "God, forgive me for _____

_____ ."

Read Psalm 66:17–20. Notice two key elements that prompted God to listen to the psalmist's prayer—worship and confession. These can often be the most neglected in our prayers today. If we are not praying regularly, we certainly are not confessing or worshipping regularly.

Many people say their prayers were not answered because it was not God's will. Perhaps that's true some of the time, but I think this can also be the easy church answer.

♥ In the following verses, what prevents prayers from being heard?

Isaiah 59:1–2

Psalm 66:18

♥ According to the following verses, what other effects can unconfessed sin have?

Genesis 3:8 and 10

Proverbs 28:13

Proverbs 29:23

Hebrews 12:6

Just a note: *Prosper* in Proverbs 28:13 does not necessarily mean to gain materially but could very well mean spiritually or even physically. It means to push forward, literally or figuratively, to break out, come mightily, to thrive.

Have you ever known someone whose sin made them sick in some way? See Psalms 32:3–4; 38:3; and 107:17 for examples.

Unconfessed sin causes us to be unhealthy spiritually and even physically. It affects our relationship with God because we tend to hide from Him when we're guilty, as Adam and Eve did. It causes God to have to discipline us. It allows pride to take root and flourish, and it causes more sin to grow like weeds in a garden that, if not plucked, can take over.

I guess ignorance is not bliss after all.

In 2 Samuel 11 and 12, we read of David's adulterous affair. If he had confessed it right away, chances are he would not have lied and schemed to cover it up, which resulted in murder and ultimately his son's death. Lingering guilt causes desensitization to our sin. Pretty soon it builds up to much worse and even can affect others. Finally, in David's case, Nathan stepped in as a good friend and mentor and held him accountable.

> For my iniquities have gone over my head; like a heavy burden, they are too heavy for me.
>
> —Psalm 38:4

Can you think of any other examples of what unconfessed sin can do, perhaps some from your own life?

I will return again to my place, until they acknowledge their guilt and seek my face, and in their distress earnestly seek me.

—Hosea 5:15

Confession changes us because it cleanses us and clears our conscience. It doesn't maintain our salvation, which is secure, but it maintains our fellowship and relationship with our Lord, our spiritual health and growth, and our witness.

However, confession of sin does not necessarily negate the physical consequences of our sin. Sometimes we still must reap what we have sown. But it sure does free us from the burden of guilt and restores our relationship with God, and often even others.

I acknowledged my sin to you, and I did not cover my iniquity; I said, "I will confess my transgressions to the LORD," and you forgave the iniquity of my sin

—Psalm 32:5

Consider your prayer life. Is there any sin hindering your prayers?

If we confess our sins, he is faithful and just to forgive us our sins and to cleanse us from all unrighteousness.

—1 John 1:9

Great job today. I *confess*, this was a tough day, but it is absolutely necessary if we're going to have an effective prayer life. See you tomorrow.

Day Two

ADJUST YOUR ACTIONS

Yet now I am happy, not because you were made sorry, but
because your sorrow led you to repentance.

—2 Corinthians 7:9 NIV

Yesterday we saw that confession means to acknowledge our sins
and agree with God as to what He says about them. In short, it
means to admit we are wrong. But we can't just acknowledge our
wrong, we must make some adjustments. We must repent.

My husband recently came home and commented, "Wow, I guess
you've been busy. The dishes are still in the sink."

"I know," I acknowledged.

I admitted to—confessed—the mess, but that didn't get it cleaned up,
washed, and returned to the cabinets.

Read 1 Samuel 7:3, and explain what Samuel told the people.

If the Israelites were truly returning to the Lord with all their heart (repentant), they would get rid of their false gods (make an adjustment) and
obey God only. Then they would be delivered out of danger. You can read
the rest of the chapter to find out what happened. (Notice the memorial
in verse 12.)

As we saw yesterday, sometimes there is sin preventing our prayers from being answered (Psalm 66:18). What happened in Ezra 9:6 as a result of a lack of repentance?

Shame and guilt are not the only things we experience as a result of not repenting. We could do a whole study on the consequences of sins that have not been dealt with. Let's look instead at an example of true repentance in 2 Corinthians 7:9–11.

What does true repentance produce?

Repentance is evidence of whether or not we possess real sorrow over our sin. It indicates whether we're just sorry for the consequences or the fact we grieved the heart of

Contrite: crushed, humbled to the point of destruction (of own will and desires)

God (Ephesians 4:30). True repentance means we make whatever adjustments need to be made and produces an earnest desire to do better.

♥ One of our verses last week was Isaiah 57:15. Look at it again and answer the question, what is necessary for a person to be truly repentant?

> For thus says the One who is high and lifted up, who inhabits eternity, whose name is Holy: "I dwell in the high and holy place, and also with him who is of a *contrite* and lowly spirit, to revive the spirit of the lowly, and to revive the heart of the *contrite*."
>
> —Isaiah 57:15 (emphasis added)

He is high and holy and yet dwells with lowly us. Let me clarify—He dwells with those whose hearts are *lowly* (contrite—humble—the opposite of being too prideful to admit when we have done wrong). He revives those who are broken over their sin (see also Psalm 34:18).

Proverbs 1:32 states, "The complacency of fools destroys them." When we ignore the Holy Spirit's conviction to confess and repent, we can risk becoming desensitized to our sin. Next we may find we no longer feel God's presence and closeness, which can lead to complete apathy if we do not respond.

Write out Revelation 3:19 below.

Those whom I _____

_____ .

> Repent therefore, and turn back, that your sins may be blotted out.
>
> —Acts 3:19

Real repentance, then, is a radical change of heart that leads to adjusting our actions accordingly. It is taking responsibility with none to blame but our own decisions and actions and returning wholeheartedly to the Lord (remember the "with all your heart" verse?).

♥ We looked at Psalm 51 in Week One. Let's look at it again, paying close attention to verses 10, 12, and 17. Summarize each verse here.

Psalm 51:10

Psalm 51:12

Psalm 51:17

How do these verses apply to repentance?

Notice they all refer to the heart or the spirit. Confession and repentance are not head things; they are heart things.

♥ What does Acts 3:19–20 say would come if we repent?

Have you ever experienced that refreshing feeling after you've sincerely confessed and repented of something? It's freeing, isn't it? Repentance is a gift, not a burden.

They say there are two sides to every coin, and there is a second side to the "forgive us our debts" part in the Lord's Prayer, and that is, "As we also have forgiven our debtors" (Matthew 6:12).

There is another adjustment we may need to make. Just as we are forgiven, we are to forgive.

According to Matthew 5:44, what are we told to do when we're offended?

In Matthew 5:23–24, what are we told to do when we give?

♥ Since this is a study about prayer, what does Mark 11:25 say we are to do when we pray? Why?

See Matthew 5:46–47. How does it relate to forgiveness?

(I know, pretty convicting.)

Let's look at how the Pharisee prayed in Luke 18:11, "The Pharisee, standing by himself, prayed thus: 'God, I thank you that I am not like other men, extortioners, unjust, adulterers, or even like this tax collector.'"

When we pray with anything against another person, aren't we indirectly saying the same thing? If we have a grudge against someone, our inner attitude is saying we're better than that person and our sin isn't as great. We must remember we all have the same sinful nature even if our sins are different.

> Forgiveness doesn't excuse their behavior. Forgiveness prevents their behavior from destroying your heart.
>
> —Justin and Trisha Davis, *Beyond Ordinary*

The following are tough verses, but they cannot be ignored. I would love to water them down and make excuses for us and let us all have a warm fuzzy fest, but I would not be doing us any favors.

♥ What do the following verses say?

Matthew 6:15

James 2:13

Simple as that. (Or maybe not.) Forgive, if you want forgiveness. Give, and it will be given to you. The measure you give will be the measure you receive (Luke 6:38).

How does Matthew 18:35 say we are to forgive?

There's that "whole heart" thing again. This is so much more than lip service. This is the real deal—genuine, authentic, no-faux forgiveness.

And then we're told to do it seventy times seven (Matthew 18:21–22)! In other words we're to give complete forgiveness as many times as is necessary. Whoa!

How do you struggle in this area?

Remember all things are possible with God and He helps us in our weakness (Romans 8:26). He is able to change hearts and heal relationships.

Note: Restored relationships are not always immediate or even achievable. Forgiving someone doesn't necessarily mean we can instantly trust them again. It doesn't always mean we let them fully back into our lives and hearts. These things are dependent on *their* repentance, which may or may not be existent and is separate from our forgiving them.

Is there someone you need His help to forgive? Ask the Lord for His help. He is faithful, and He is able, if we are willing.

Like all acts of obedience, forgiveness is a choice not a feeling. If we obey, feelings will follow. Every time I've asked God to change my heart, He supernaturally and faithfully did. You will never be sorry for forgiving someone, but the opposite will likely hold true. Unforgiveness will keep us in prison while the other person walks free.

> Sometimes you might be tempted to say, "But you don't know what they did to me! You don't know how bad they hurt me!" Aren't you glad God doesn't say that when we come to Him? What terror would it cause if suddenly we heard from heaven, "No forgiveness today. I'll have nothing to do with you. You have no idea how badly you've hurt Me." Instead, He loves and forgives us—and expects us to treat others with the same compassion.
>
> —Kay Arthur, David Lawson, and B. J. Lawson, *The Essentials of Effective Prayer*

According to Psalm 51:4 who are their offenses really against?

Jesus' act of forgiveness on the Cross is the reason we are to forgive others, no matter what they've done. Jesus took the punishment for every sin you and I and our offenders have ever committed. Isaiah 53:5–6 says, "He was pierced for our transgressions, crushed for our iniquities, chastised for our peace, and *all* our iniquities were laid on Him" (paraphrase mine).

That should be reason itself for us to be able to forgive others, especially their often-petty grievances. But sometimes it's good to hear how someone else handles a hard situation. So I'd like to share my friend Jessica's forgiveness story. It's a wonderful testimony to the possibility and power of forgiveness and a true "love thy neighbor" story.

Two days after Jessica and her husband purchased their dream home, things turned into a nightmare when their neighbor began disputing boundaries. This neighbor went to great lengths to drive them from their new home. The neighbor tormented them by photographing them and their guests, painting red lines in the middle of the driveway, cutting off their access to phone and internet, and even trying to defame Jessica's character at her workplace.

They began to fear what would happen next as things went from bad to worse, eventually leading to court hearings and lawsuits. As Jessica prayed and contemplated how to love her neighbor in the midst of defending their rights, she realized everything was useless except relying on God to miraculously resolve the conflict.

Jessica had been praying God would get the glory, but through prayer realized she was to *give* God the glory. She realized she was to love selflessly even though she had been hurt so deeply.

It was then things began to change.

Jessica called the harassing neighbor and invited her to breakfast. (Really, who does that?) What two years of mediation with attorneys and the court system had been unable to resolve, God began to change during that four-hour conversation.

To make a long story short, Jessica and her husband ended up purchasing the neighbor's property, and the neighbor moved out of the area—with an open invitation to visit each other any time!

Jessica gives God all the glory for how He worked things out when nothing else could.

How did Jessica adjust her actions, which led to resolution?

Remember, none of this comes close to how much Jesus forgave us. How can Jesus' forgiveness, suffering, and sacrifice on the Cross help you to forgive others?

The test of a true Christ-follower is mercy. As Christ said in the Sermon on the Mount, "Blessed are the merciful, for they shall receive mercy" (Matthew 5:7).

Day Three

AVOID TEMPTATION

And lead us not into temptation, but deliver us from evil.

—Matthew 6:13

Welcome back. You're doing great with these difficult topics. Tomorrow we'll talk about God's amazing grace, but for now we're going to talk about temptation.

We all face temptation. We may be tempted to cheat, covet, or cuss on a daily basis. So what can we do?

Jesus taught us to pray against temptation and evil. It is part of His model prayer, so He must want us to pay attention to it.

The very words of Matthew 6:13 imply spiritual warfare is a reality. Why would we need to be delivered from an evil enemy if he doesn't exist? He is real, he is evil, and he lives to tempt us and bait us into sin. First Peter 5:8 tells us to be sober-minded and watchful because our adversary the devil prowls around like a roaring lion seeking to devour us.

Let's look at the first part of today's verse, "Lead us not into temptation."

On the tempt-o-meter you see here, mark where you think you are in your "temptometric" pressure.

The word *temptation* can be interpreted as a test or trial. Certainly, any temptation tries our spiritual character and tests our strength to resist.

♥ While God may allow certain tests or trials in our life, who does James 1:13 say does not *tempt* us? What *does* tempt us (v. 14)?

♥ What does John say about where our desires come from in 1 John 2:16?

Note: You may want to keep in mind while doing this lesson that Jesus referred to Satan as the "ruler of this world" in John 14:30. (You may also see this in 2 Corinthians 4:4; Ephesians 2:2; 1 John 4:4; and 5:19.)

♥ In Matthew 4:1, who tempted Jesus?

So it is not God who temps us, but *we* who are enticed by our own desires, which Satan dangles in front of us to lead us to sin. We could interpret this part of the Lord's Prayer as: *Lord, help me not to give in to wrong desires and have to be tested.*

♥ Satan even tried to tempt Jesus with desires. What desires do you see used in Matthew 4:2–11?

The first temptation is fleshly hunger. Of course, this is not a bad desire; we all need to eat (unless, of course, it becomes gluttony). But why do you think Satan used this temptation with Jesus (verse 2)?

Whenever we are committed to doing something for God, Satan tries to sabotage it, particularly at our weakest point, and especially when we fast and pray. (We'll discuss fasting in Week Six.)

The second temptation relates to pride and power, and the third the lust of the eyes, all of which are familiar desires to us.

How do you see Satan's craving for power running through all of the temptations?

How did Jesus resist these temptations in Matthew 4:4, 7, and 10?

It's imperative to know the Word. Temptation is not the sin but rather the acting upon it. We alone are responsible for our actions, even though Satan has been using our desires against us since Adam and Eve. They didn't want to take responsibility for their actions either. Eve blamed the serpent, and then Adam blamed Eve and even God. They invented the classic blame game. But though they were tempted and deceived by Satan, they had a choice. They could either give in to their desires or resist. And we have the same choice. "Resist the devil," James 4:7 tells us, "and he will flee from you."

♥ Look up Deuteronomy 30:19. See the choice God gave us all, and fill in the blanks below.

I have set before you _____ and _____, _____ and _____. Therefore, choose _____.

♥ Furthermore, God provided offensive weapons for us. What are they according to the following verses?

Ephesians 6:17

Romans 8:26

The Apostle Paul prayed for the Ephesians that they would "understand the incredible greatness of God's power for us who believe him. This is the same mighty power that raised Christ from the dead" (Ephesians 1:19–20 NLT). If you have received Jesus Christ as your Lord and Savior, the same power that raised Jesus from the dead lives in *you*. Think about that. What does this mean for you?

What did Paul say to "put on" for help in Romans 13:14? (See also Ephesians 4:24.)

Notice he said to put Christ on so they would "make no provision for the flesh, to gratify its desires." That's like saying, "don't allow yourself to be led into temptation." This "putting on" protects us as clothing protects our bodies, or more aptly, how the armor protects the Christian (Ephesians 6:13–18).

To *put on* or *clothe* oneself with Christ is to put Him on as our armor, just as you would get dressed each day. It implies closeness, just as our clothing is against our skin. Furthermore, it is to exchange His thoughts and behavior for ours, as though we take off one set of clothing and put on another.

Who are we to walk with and why according to Galatians 5:16?

> To *walk by* or *in* means as the spirit guides, with His help, by His rule for ultimate victory. The word *walk* denotes activity and therefore implies continual walking in the spirit.

So we put Christ's clothing on and walk with Him through our life's journey in order to attain victory over temptation and sin.

Let's move on to the second part of this verse in the Lord's Prayer: "but deliver us from evil."

The word *deliver* comes from the Greek word *rhuomai,* meaning to rescue, snatch from danger, save or set free, and even to drag. An image of a soldier dragging his comrade to safety comes to my mind.

The word *evil* can be interpreted "evil one" or "evil spirits," as we see in other versions. Jesus not only taught us to pray to be delivered from the evil one, He prayed this Himself for us in John 17:15, "[I ask] that you keep them from the evil one."

When we pray, "Deliver us from evil," it's like saying, "Please rescue me, drag me if you have to, from Satan and his angels."

Has God ever had to drag you out of your temptation or sin? Explain.

How often do you pray, not just rote words in the Lord's Prayer but actually pray against temptation and evil in your life? In the world?

First Peter 2:11 tells us the passions of the flesh "wage war" against our souls. Most women don't like violence or fighting. I think it's safe to say we would choose a chick flick over a war movie. But when we became a Christian, we entered the spiritual military, and unless we attend spiritual boot camp and participate in ongoing training, we will not be prepared for the inevitable fights involved with spiritual warfare. Preparation and training is ongoing in military life, and it's necessary in the Christian life also. That's why Paul tells us in Ephesians 6:13–18 to *put on* the full armor of God.

Notice the armor in Ephesians 6 covers only the front. Perhaps this is because we are not supposed to turn our back on the battle. Turning away will leave us unprotected.

So suit up, warrior!

♥ Who does Ephesians 6:12 say we war, or struggle, with?

You may wonder what all those words mean in Ephesians 6:12—rulers, authorities, powers, etc. Here's a brief explanation:

- Rulers (principalities, NKJV) (*archas*): Beginning, rule; the first person or thing in a series, the leader; angels and demons holding dominions entrusted to them in the order of things
- Authorities (powers, NKJV) (*exousias*): authority; dominion; jurisdiction; delegated authority; the leading and more powerful among created beings superior to man, spiritual potentates
- Cosmic Powers (rulers, NKJV) (*kosmokratór*): world ruler; the world asserting its independence of God; used of the angelic or demonic

powers controlling the sublunary world; referring to Satan (demons) influencing the lives of worldly people

- This Present Darkness (darkness of this age, NKJV) (*skotos*): either physical or moral darkness; the principle of sin with its certain results; has the power of rendering men bold to commit crimes; shadiness
- Evil (wickedness, NKJV) (*ponéria*): iniquity, wickedness, pain-ridden evil, malice, depravity
- Heavenly Places (*epouranios*): in the heavenly sphere, the sphere of spiritual activities; celestial

What the Apostle Paul is teaching is there is an unseen spiritual war going on, and our battles are ultimately spiritual in nature. Our war is against Satan and his angels. However we have a Spirit in us who is much more powerful than those forces of evil. But we must *choose* His help. Richard Foster wrote in his book *Prayer: Finding the Heart's True Home*, "But remember, we are told that the gates of hell cannot withstand the onslaughts of the Church (Matthew 16:18). The kingdom of darkness goes into full retreat when we take up the full weapons of our warfare." (See also Ephesians 1:19–21.)

♥ In addition to the offensive weapons we talked about earlier, God also provided defensive weapons for us to *put on* in Ephesians 6:13–18. What are they?

Just as in the military you wouldn't go to war without your rifle loaded, you cannot expect to win battles against the devil's army without your spiritual weapons loaded and ready to use. The Bible is an armory full of spiritual weapons.

We saw how Jesus handled Satan with knowledge and skill. If it is true many Christians are not regularly in the Word and prayer, then we are living dangerously unprepared and oblivious to the enemy. How do the troubles in our world attest to the idea that we have not been mindful of the enemy or taken him seriously enough?

I shared with you how I felt God impressed on me the church has been sleeping, much like the disciples were when Jesus asked them to pray. What did Jesus tell His followers in Matthew 26:41 and why?

In Ephesians 6:18, Paul instructs us to be in prayer, to keep alert (or watchful, NKJV), and to have perseverance. But we cannot be watchful if we do not know what the Word says to watch for. Are you spiritually awake, watchful, and prayerful? If not, we will be too weak to persevere in avoiding temptation.

We have a very potent enemy who wants to remain unnoticed and is too often ignored. Therefore he easily gains the advantage over us. How would you say this is true/untrue in our society today? In your life?

My oldest son served in the United States Marine Corps. They have extensive classroom training as well as rigorous physical training. They are also trained to know their weapons inside and out. They must take their rifle apart, clean it, and put it back together hundreds of times so they know it as well as they know their name and can use it in the dark or immediately react under any kind of pressure.

Our classroom training is the Word of God. Prayer is our physical training. Our weapons are the pieces of armor in Ephesians 6. Just as in the military, we must have all three to be fully knowledgeable, proficiently skilled, and masterfully prepared to defend ourselves (and others) against the enemy's schemes.

Though we walk in the flesh, we are not waging war according to the flesh. For the weapons of our warfare are not of the flesh but have divine power to destroy strongholds.

—2 Corinthians 10:3–4

Charles Spurgeon said, "We are not merely to defend, but also to assail. It is not enough that you are not conquered; you have to conquer: and hence we find, that we are to take, not only a helmet to protect the head, but also a sword, with which to annoy the foe" (*Twelve Sermons on Spiritual Warfare*). Is the enemy annoyed by you? Or are you no threat to him? Explain.

In Matthew 3:3, John the Baptist preached, "Prepare the way of the Lord; make his paths straight." When we repent and adjust our lives, including forgiving others and avoiding temptation, our paths become straight and we make a way for the Lord to work. Then we are able to experience the abundant life Jesus spoke of in John 10:10.

I hope you've progressed well this week with this tough subject. I'm so proud of you for hanging in there. I trust you've come through better equipped. Tomorrow we end the week on a more inspiring note. I'm excited to study God's amazing grace, aren't you?

We wouldn't even be able to pray, "Deliver us from evil," if it weren't for grace.

Blessed is the man who endures temptation; for when he has been approved, he will receive the crown of life which the Lord has promised to those who love Him.

—James 1:12 NKJV

Day Four

ACCEPT HIS AMAZING GRACE

Where sin increased, grace abounded all the more.

—Romans 5:20

Once we have acknowledged our sin, asked forgiveness, and adjusted our lives, we can accept His amazing grace. So today, let's spend some time immersed in His grace, which comes from the Greek word *charis,* meaning gift, acceptance, kindness. It is the same word as *favor* or *a favor.*

♥ Romans 5:1–2 says, "Therefore, since we have been justified by faith, we have peace with God through our Lord Jesus Christ. Through him we have also obtained access by faith into this grace in which we now stand." Where do you stand today? Are you standing on that grace, or do you feel unworthy to stand on such holy ground?

Many people don't fully comprehend the concept of grace and continue to have feelings of guilt even after salvation. If you have sincerely asked forgiveness, you immediately received God's grace—His unmerited favor, unearned, undeserved, yet freely and completely given. Still others feel they need to *do* something to earn His grace.

Romans 3:28 states, "For we hold that one is justified by faith apart from works of the law." The word *justified* is from the Greek word *dikaioó*, which means to plead for, justify, render innocent, to make righteous.

It's like being acquitted, cleared of all charges, made free. This means that if we are justified or forgiven of sin, then it's as though we've never even sinned in the first place. Or as Psalm 103:12 tells us, "As far as the east is from the west, so far does he remove our transgressions from us."

♥ Read Titus 3:5 below. Circle what grants us His grace, and cross out where grace does not come from.

> He saved us, not because of works done by us in righteousness, but according to his own mercy, by the washing of regeneration and renewal of the Holy Spirit.

How good are you at resting in the assurance that you can do nothing to earn His grace?

Because I mess up so often, sometimes it's easier for me to tell others about God's love and grace than it has been to believe it for myself. But it is the disease of sin itself for which we are forgiven, and for which we have little control over and can do nothing about apart from God's grace. Once I realized God's grace covered my sin *nature*, not just my sins, I experienced the freedom expressed in 2 Corinthians 3:17: "Now the Lord is the Spirit, and where the Spirit of the Lord is, there is freedom."

Are you experiencing the freedom of His forgiveness and grace? How are you experiencing the grace of God, not just in salvation, but in daily, grace-filled living like we see in 1 Timothy 1:14, "And the grace of our Lord overflowed for me with the faith and love that are in Christ Jesus"?

Your cup of grace is not half empty. It is full to overflowing! Psalm 23:5 says, "My cup overflows." As we continually ask forgiveness, He continually pours out His grace.

Many of us would like a fresh start in several areas of our lives. Lamentations 3:23 says His mercies "are new every morning." We get a fresh slate to write on each day. There's no need to brood over yesterday's mistakes. We can't change things we've done, but we can have new mercies for them.

No matter how undeserving we are, Hebrews 4:16 invites us, "Let us then with confidence draw near to the throne of *grace*, that we may receive mercy" (emphasis added). Because, as we read in Revelation 21:5, He makes all things new.

Why would we not accept such an invitation? Perhaps if we really comprehended grace, we would have the confidence to come more often and more boldly. (See this week's activity for further study for a deeper understanding of God's grace and mercy.)

♥ Read Paul's confession in Acts 26:9–16 and 1 Timothy 1:14–17. Contrast his sinfulness and God's grace. What was Paul's focus?

I see Paul focused on God's grace and purpose, not on his sin, which would have kept him stuck and not doing what God purposed for him to do. Paul tells about his sin, not with guilt but to glorify God for His forgiveness. His whole focus shifted from vehemently persecuting Christians to passionately telling everyone he could about God's amazing grace.

Imagine if instead he focused on who he *used to be* and believed the enemy's lie that God could never use him because his sin had been so great. Even as I write this, I realize how silly it sounds. If you know anything about the Apostle Paul, you know he did just the opposite. He did not allow the enemy to use his history to keep him from his destiny. Yet that's not the case for too many of us.

♥ Contrast sin and grace as explained in Romans 5:20.

It's not about us. It's about *Him* and what He has done for you and me. He saved us, not because of anything good we may have done but because of the good He has done for us on the Cross. That's grace. And He saved us in spite of and no matter how bad we may have been. That's mercy.

How fully are you living in the assurance of His grace?

If you still need assurance that His grace is enough, take some time to meditate on the following verses, praying and thanking God for His grace.

> I, I am He who blots out your transgressions for my own sake, and I will not remember your sins.
>
> —Isaiah 43:25

> He will again have compassion on us; he will tread our iniquities underfoot. You will cast all our sins into the depths of the sea.
>
> —Micah 7:19

> For sin will have no dominion over you, since you are not under law but under grace.
>
> —Romans 6:14

There is therefore now no condemnation for those who are in Christ Jesus.

—Romans 8:1

In him we have redemption through his blood, the forgiveness of our trespasses, according to the riches of his grace, which he lavished upon us.

—Ephesians 1:7–8

The grace of our Lord overflowed for me with the faith and love that are in Christ Jesus.

—1 Timothy 1:14

Which one of the previous verses means the most to you and why?

You've made it through to the halfway point of our study. I pray you've come away from this week feeling forgiven, free, and filled with His amazing grace. Now may "the grace of the Lord Jesus Christ and the love of God and the fellowship of the Holy Spirit be with you all" (2 Corinthians 13:14).

For Further Study

ACCEPTED INTO HIS THRONE ROOM

Let us therefore come boldly to the throne of grace, that we may obtain mercy and find grace to help in time of need.

—Hebrews 4:16 NKJV

As stated in Week One, prayer is a privilege. First Peter 2:7 claims it's an honor to come to Him. Verse 9 calls believers a "royal priesthood."

This is because in the Old Testament, the high priest was the only one allowed to enter the Holy of Holies, the innermost area of the Tabernacle, to make sacrifices for the people's sins.

The Holy of Holies held the Ark of the Covenant, which represented God's presence. The area was separated from the rest of the Tabernacle by a massive, heavy curtain, sixty feet high by thirty feet wide and about four inches thick. This "veil" of blue, purple, and scarlet finely twisted linen represented the separation sin had created between the people and God, who is too holy to look upon sin. It reminded the people they could not enter God's presence carelessly or irreverently.

Once a year on the Day of Atonement the high priest entered with his head bowed so he would not look upon God's presence. He interceded for the people and prayed specific prayers. With great fear, he lifted the corner of the veil to place the blood of the sacrifice on top of the Ark, which was called the Mercy Seat. Then he backed out, so as to not turn His back on God.

However, God desired our relationship more than our sacrifices. In love, He came to us in the person of Jesus Christ and in mercy offered Himself as the only once-for-all sacrifice for our sins. Jesus sprinkled His own blood on the Mercy Seat. And at the very moment He breathed His last breath on the Cross, as a person in mourning would tear his garments, God tore the curtain in two from top to bottom (impossible for man to do).

There is now no separation between God and man. The massive split in the veil now creates an ample opening for the greatest sinners to approach God and receive His mercy and love. The veil now represents Jesus' body, torn for us.

Believers are now fully and eternally forgiven and have free access to God. We can speak to God as a child speaks with his or her father.

Mercy Seat (*kapporeth*)—covering, as to cover over sin; atonement

We no longer need any priest or man to mediate between God and us. We are all priests, and Jesus is our High Priest, forever interceding for us. No one comes to the Father except through Jesus Christ (John 14:6).

Jesus said in John 16:24, "Until now you have asked nothing in my name. Ask, and you will receive, that your joy may be full." To ask in His name is to ask in His *authority*. We now have the authority only the high priest once had. "Until now"—now that He has offered forgiveness through His blood; now that you do not need the high priest to make sacrifices for you; now that God's presence, the Holy Spirit, lives in you.

Now we can "come boldly to the throne of grace." Nothing can separate us now, except us.

Knowing the freedom and privilege we now have and the price Jesus paid, why would we not come boldly and come often?

Therefore, brothers, since we have confidence to enter the holy places by the blood of Jesus, by the new and living way that he opened for us through the curtain, that is, through his flesh, and since we have a great priest over the house of God, let us draw near with a true heart in full assurance of faith, with our hearts sprinkled clean from an evil conscience and our bodies washed with pure water.

—Hebrews 10:19–22

Day Five

WEEK IN REVIEW

If I had cherished iniquity in my heart, the Lord would not have
listened. But truly God has listened; he has attended
to the voice of my prayer.

—Psalm 66:18–19

Acknowledge Sin and Ask Forgiveness

Adjust Your Actions

Avoid Temptation

Accept His Amazing Grace

For All Participants:

Contemplate—What did you learn this week, and what was a reminder?

Consider—What might it cost you to not continually confess and repent?

Commit—What action might you need to take in order to have a more effective prayer life?

Write a prayer to God considering all you've studied this week.

For Individuals:

Go back through the week's sessions and reread anything you may have highlighted, and review the ♥ questions.

Session Three Leader Guide for Groups:

Welcome attendees back. Pray to open.

Invite anyone who would like to briefly share a time when another person forgave them.

Go over Week Three ♥ questions together, as well as the contemplate-consider-commit questions, if you have time.

Watch Video Y and discuss.

Take prayer requests (remember to keep it short so everyone can share), and close in prayer.

WEEK FOUR

Y

Yield to His Will

Theme: Discovering the blessings that come from seeking God's kingdom and His will for our lives.

Day One

YOUR KINGDOM COME

Your kingdom come.

—Matthew 6:10

Welcome to Week Four. Week Three was a tough one for me. How about you?

Christianity sure isn't for the fainthearted. I hope you were blessed by ending the week focusing on God's amazing grace. It's His grace that has carried us this far, in our life and in this study.

This week, we will address the "your kingdom come, your will be done" portion of the Lord's Prayer. The Y this week then is for yield—yielding our will to His.

Sin and God's will are tough subjects, so I want to encourage you not to miss any of the blessings God has for you as you pursue a deeper relationship with Him through this study.

Today we will focus on the first part, "Your kingdom come." Just what does this mean? We're not used to speaking in terms of kingdoms, except maybe the Magic Kingdom at Walt Disney World. We don't have a king in the United States; we have a president. And we don't say we live in a kingdom; we say we live in a country.

Or perhaps you've heard the expression, "from here to kingdom come," as my mom used to say.

"Kingdom of God" and "kingdom of heaven" are used interchangeably by the writers of Scripture. It may be that some used the word *heaven* because Jews did not like to use the word *God* for fear of disrespecting His name.

If you have access to a concordance, look up "kingdom of God" and "king-dom of heaven." How many references can you find?

"Kingdom of God/heaven" is used repeatedly in the New Testament. My own count totalled close to one hundred. In the Gospel of Matthew I counted more than thirty occurrences.

A king has the highest position of power. Furthermore, kingship is an inherited, lifelong position. The word *kingdom* (*basileia*) means sovereignty, authority, power, and dominion. *Basileia* is constantly used in connection with the rule of Christ in the hearts of believers. Even Merriam-Webster tells us it's the realm in which God's will is fulfilled. Does this help you understand *your kingdom come*?

♥ What do you learn about His kingdom in the following verses?

Daniel 7:14

Luke 1:33 and 21:28–31

Matthew 4:17 and 25:34

God's kingdom is timeless and eternal just as He is eternal. We are told in Psalm 145:13, "Your kingdom is an everlasting kingdom, and your dominion endures through all generations."

What reason did Jesus give for coming in Luke 4:43 and John 18:37?

But if Jesus already brought God's kingdom, why do we have to pray for it to come?

Jesus brought, made available, His kingdom here on earth, but it is up to us to submit to it, to invite it into our hearts and lives. When we pray, "Your kingdom come . . . on earth as it is in heaven," we are inviting His rule on earth and in our lives to accomplish His sovereign, righteous purposes. We become His kingdom on earth.

Furthermore the Jews' constant prayer was for their prophesied, long-awaited Messiah to come, so "your kingdom come" was a prayer they could relate to. The Jews Jesus spoke to in Matthew 6 were accustomed to earthly kings who dominated and oppressed the poor while exploiting and favoring the rich. They wanted a quick fix and hoped for a political king who would free them from Rome's bondage. But Jesus spoke of a spiritual kingdom where the Messiah would rule with mercy, justice, and love and reign supreme and victorious, not just for them in that time but for future generations, all races, and for all eternity.

God answered their prayer. There He was, the Messiah bringing the kingdom of God right into their presence, and they didn't see it.

Do *you* see it?

Have you ever been like the Israelites: wanting His kingdom your way, your idea of what His kingdom should be like? Give examples.

For to us a child is born, to us a son is given; and the government shall be upon his shoulder, and his name shall be called Wonderful Counselor, Mighty God, Everlasting Father, Prince of Peace. Of the increase of his government and of peace there will be no end, on the throne of David and over his kingdom, to establish it and to uphold it with justice and with righteousness from this time forth and forevermore. The zeal of the LORD of hosts will do this.

—Isaiah 9:6–7

What is heaven's kingdom like on earth? The disciples asked Jesus this question, and He answered them using many different parables (a story using symbolism to teach a point). Choose one or more passages and summarize what Jesus said the kingdom of God is like. What do these mean to you personally?

Matthew 13:1–9, 18–23

Matthew 13:24–33

Matthew 13:44–46

Matthew 13:47–50

Another reason Jesus came was to destroy the works of the devil—to destroy Satan's kingdom in this world and establish God's kingdom to overcome it (1 John 3:8).

♥ Who is this kingdom for? (See John 1:12; John 11:52; 1 John 5:1.)

In Matthew 5:3, who are the blessed, and what will they receive?

Remember Week Three when we talked about a contrite heart? That is what it means to be poor in spirit. The word *poor* in this sense (*ptóchos*) means one who cowers, beggarly, to be conscious of spiritual need and destitute for eternal riches (see Revelation 3:17). The word *blessed* (*makarios*) on the other hand means happy, fortunate; even an enviable position from obeying and receiving God's provisions and grace. This is because of the kingdom's benefits we inherit by believing in and receiving our King.

Those who are humble (poor) see their need for God's salvation. They are willing to submit to His kingdom authority and receive the favor (blessing) of His heavenly kingdom in their hearts, lives, and in their eternity.

Where did Jesus say in Luke 17:20–21 and John 14:16–17 the kingdom of God is?

When Christ's kingdom is in you, what is its effect (Colossians 1:27)?

What does Romans 14:17 say the kingdom of God is not, and what does it say it is?

The kingdom of God is not tangible but spiritual.

When I think of kings I think of opulence and riches. What are some of the rich spiritual blessings of *His* kingdom in the following verses?

Ephesians 1:7

Philippians 4:19

What might some of the needs referred to in Philippians 4:19 be, considering Galatians 5:22–23?

And what are some of the needs, considering Colossians 2:2–3?

Refer back to the names of God we looked at in Week Two, Day Four and the words you listed to describe Him. Isn't that the kind of king you want over the kingdom of your life?

♥ Finally, look at the following verses and consider the ways earth becomes more like heaven.

Matthew 28:19–20

John 13:34–35

Acts 1:8

Colossians 3:16

James 5:16

What governs you? What governs most of your priorities, time, and energy? Is it mostly temporary and perishable earthly things or valuable and lasting kingdom things?

What are some ways you can begin to allow God's kingdom to reign foremost in your life?

Let's ask Jesus to come be His kingdom on earth and in our hearts. Let that be our ultimate desire. As it is in heaven, so be it in us.

Lord, I pray, let Your kingdom come into the hearts of men and women everywhere. Let Your kingdom come into the hearts of our loved ones and friends. Let Your kingdom come!

He has delivered us from the domain of darkness and transferred us to the kingdom of his beloved Son, in whom we have redemption, the forgiveness of sins.

—Colossians 1:13–14

Day Two

Your Will Be Done

Your will be done, on earth as it is in heaven.

—Matthew 6:10

Have you heard the story of the rebellious child who, when made to sit in the corner, told his mother he was still standing up on the inside? Ever felt like that? Though our heads are bowed and our hands are folded, we're really asking for our will to be done, not His.

I don't know which is more difficult—acknowledging our sins or yielding to His will. Which do you think is more difficult and why?

Pursuing God in prayer, remembering to worship Him, and acknowledging and confessing our sins are all part of *yielding*—lining up our lives with His kingdom and will. As we submit our will and desires to His, delighting in Him, we end up fulfilling the desires of our hearts (Psalm 37:4). Are you seeing how all these things work together?

I've heard that prayer releases God's power. True prayer not only submits to His will, it *invites* it. It's like saying, "Lord, You are free to work according to Your will in this situation."

Who's in control anyway? We humans *want* to be in control, but we've never had any control to begin with. Human control is a delusion. So why not trust your life to the One who *is* in control and knows your beginning and end and everything in between?

When we pray for His will over our own, trusting that He has everything under control and in our best interests (Matthew 6:8), our desires become His desires and are therefore met. To yield is to "seek first the kingdom of God and his righteousness, and all these things will be added to you" (v. 33).

Yielding is not easy. We don't naturally want God's will. In the flesh, we want our own way. Even once we become believers, for many it's a process to accept His will over ours. We want to be in control, but our control hinders God's will

> What the praying man does is to bring his will into line with the will of God so God can do what He has all along been willing to do.
>
> —A. W. Tozer, *Prayer*

and work in our lives because it puts our will—our agenda—above His. And we risk jeopardizing our own good when we insist on our own way.

We all have done it—tried to control things or people in our lives. Surrender is hard. It's part of our human nature to "do it my way." Some of us just need to let go of the need to control our world.

Who are we trusting in if we are being controlling?

If we are controlling, to whose will are we yielding?

On whose wisdom are we depending?

Does the clay say to the one who forms it, "What are you making?"

—Isaiah 45:9

Be completely honest with yourself, and finish these sentences:

I am having trouble trusting God's will for _____ .

By my own will, I have been trying to control _____ .

In Psalm 13:1–4 (NLT), David begins by repeatedly asking, "How long?" and pleads, "Turn and answer me." Yet in verses 5 and 6, he concludes with: "But I trust . . . I will rejoice . . . I will sing."

> **The word for *pray* (*proseuchomai*) literally means to exchange our wishes for His.**

Notice the repeated *I will*. No matter what David felt, he *decided*, "I will" praise God. That's yielding. He turned *my will* into *His will*.

In Psalm 56:3–4, what did David do when he was fearful?

One day my seven-year-old granddaughter complained, "Mommy always gets what she wants," meaning she always has to do what Mommy says. (Good job, Mommy.) She doesn't yet understand that what Mommy wants is what's best for her, that what Mommy says is both good and loving.

> **Yield: relinquish control**
>
> **Surrender: stop resisting; submit**

God is ultimately going to get what He wants too. We can resist it, or we can trust that what He wills is what's best for us, no matter how much we don't like it at the time. "My counsel shall stand, and I will accomplish all my purpose" (Isaiah 46:10).

You can trust your Heavenly Daddy to do what's best for you. Submit to Him. You *can* trust Him.

Fill in the blanks to complete Psalm 119:68:

You are _____ and do _____ .

As one of my favorite pastors used to recite, "God is good all the time," and the congregation would respond, "And all the time God is good."

What did God say in Genesis 1:31?

According to Ecclesiastes 7:29, what did man do?

What choice was given in Genesis 2:17?

What did man choose in Genesis 3:6?

What was the result according to Romans 8:22?

God created everything good. Man chose otherwise when he thought his own will and ideas were better than God's. God's ultimate goal is for our best, but sometimes, because of our stubborn, controlling nature, He has to allow some pretty hard stuff to get us there.

It's all part of the choice God has given to us. Do we want the ultimate blessing that comes with His perfect will and plan, or do we want to do it on our own, complete with whatever complications that may include? God doesn't force His will on us. He gives us free choice. When we pray *Your will be done*, we choose to yield to His plan instead of our own. We accept it into existence.

Adam and Eve, who represent us all, chose their way and their will over God's. We have been doing the same thing and suffering the consequences ever since—sometimes directly and sometimes indirectly because of other people's choices in this now-fallen world. We, like Adam and Eve, blame everyone else and even God for the consequences of our sin. But God only wants good for us. It is not His fault. He warned. We chose our way.

This is the good part—according to Colossians 1:19–23, what did God do to remedy the situation?

I don't know about you, but I get excited reading that. God's good will is that no one will perish (2 Peter 3:9) because of our choice to go our own way. In His mercy and grace He came to us in the person of Jesus Christ and took the punishment for all our sins on the Cross to reconcile us to Him. Wow—*that* is good!

Last week we looked at Deuteronomy 30:19. Let's look at it again. What is the choice given and God's will for our choice?

His ultimate will is that we would make life-giving choices. What choices might you have made that directly or indirectly relate to your circumstances? Have you ever suffered the consequences of your own or someone else's choices?

We must *believe* He is good and His will is good. We must *trust* that anything He allows is ultimately for our good. That's hard, especially when we're hurting. But the more time we spend with Him in His Word and prayer, the more we begin to trust Him as we learn more of Him.

What good do the following verses say our trials can produce?

Romans 5:3–5

Hebrews 12:11

James 1:2–4

God wants us to lack nothing! So ask yourself these questions: Do I trust Him? Do I believe He is trustworthy?

Psalm 125:1 says, "Those who trust in the LORD are like Mount Zion, which cannot be moved, but abides forever." This means when we really trust Him, we are immovable. We are steady, unshakable, and quietly remain that way always.

Author Ken Hemphill states in *The Prayer of Jesus*, "When we attempt to manage our own kingdom affairs, we become fretful and anxious because we have no power to control all the situations that come about or to alter our circumstances. Jesus understands this: 'Who of you by worrying can add a single hour to his life?' (Matthew 6:27 NIV). So in response He gives us an offer we should be unable to refuse: *You focus on My kingdom, and I in turn will manage your kingdom.*"

When the things of His kingdom are established in our hearts, then we allow His divine will to be fulfilled in our lives and therefore on earth. For whenever God's will is allowed to reign, His kingdom is come.

♥ Can you imagine if His name was hallowed (made holy) and His will was done in the hearts of people everywhere? What would that look like to you? In the world? In your life?

I think it would look like heaven, His kingdom come. When His name is hallowed, people see and come to know Him, which is His will. Then His kingdom is here on earth. *Oh dear Father, let it be so!*

Thy will be done should be the desire of our hearts and the goal of our prayers. We'll discuss how to know God's will tomorrow. See you then!

Day Three

YOUR WILL BE KNOWN

Look carefully then how you walk, not as unwise but as wise,
making the best use of the time, because the days are evil.
Therefore do not be foolish, but understand what the
will of the Lord is.

—Ephesians 5:15–17

esterday we talked about accepting God's will over our own. But how do we know God's will beyond His desire for all men to know the truth and to be saved, as stated in 1 Timothy 2:4, which says, "[God our Savior] desires all people to be saved and to come to the knowledge of the truth"?

Tomorrow we will talk about how to know God's specific will for your life personally, but first let's be clear about God's general will.

God's will is laid out in His Word, the Bible. God's Word is His testament, His purposes and plans, His will. It's like when we make a last will and testament, which is a statement of our desires of what we want done with our valuables after our death and what meant most to us in life.

We fulfill the will of God when we keep His commandments in His Word. The kingdom of heaven is a place where His will is unchallenged, and earth is made more like it is in heaven when we do His will and keep His commandments.

There are many Scripture passages that are basic to knowing God's general will. Let's examine several of them.

What do the following verses tell us about God's will?

John 14:15

1 John 2:3–4

On what does Philippians 4:8 say we should focus our attention?

How can you focus on these things in the situations you face today?

Next, list what Galatians 5:22–23 says should characterize us.

How are such things acquired?

This fruit is the result of His Spirit living and active inside of us. It is His will that we increasingly exhibit these qualities in our life. When we do, we will focus on what is true, honorable, etc. Then, we will make earth a little more *as it is in heaven*.

Describe what Micah 6:8 says the Lord requires (wills) of us.

When I wrote Micah 6:8 in my own words, I wrote *God's will is to do what is right and fair to others, to be merciful (forgiving) and kind, and to walk with God in humility, knowing His ways and will are higher and better than my own.*

I love how that verse starts out, "He has told you . . . what is *good*." Choose good. Choose life. That is His will, and it is for our good.

What does Romans 12:2 encourage in order to attain God's will?

When we do not conform to the world's ways and in humility seek hard after God's ways, our mind will be transformed; we will more easily think about what is good, honorable, just, etc.; we will be more merciful and kind; we will be characterized by the fruit of His Spirit.

What is His will in the following verses?

Matthew 28:19–20

John 13:34–35

Romans 10:17; 2 Timothy 3:16–17

James 1:27

James 5:16

2 Peter 3:9

Certainly this list is not exhaustive, but it gives a good idea of the things God wills for all of us—to love one another and share the gospel, increase our faith and be equipped by reading His Word, to take care of the needy, not let the world influence us to sin, to confess our sins and pray, and ultimately for all people to be saved—all ways we bring His kingdom to earth.

It is important to point out we do not become these things overnight, but we should be in a continual growth pattern.

Fill in the blanks to complete 1 Thessalonians 4:3.

This is the _____ of God, your _____.

Sanctification comes from a Greek word *hagiasmos,* which refers to the process of growing in holiness. To be sanctified is to be transformed to be holy. Therefore His will is for us to be made holy as He is holy (1 Peter 1:15–16). God is patient with us but desires to change us from the inside out. As our mind is transformed, we become more holy (and further bring God's kingdom to earth).

> **You have need of endurance, so that when you have done the will of God you may receive what is promised.**
>
> **—Hebrews 10:36**

We all need God's help in these areas. Remember, we were born with the sinful nature inherited from Adam and Eve. But God's spirit helps us in the sanctification process. The Holy Spirit is our helper (John 14:16) if we will but call on Him in each situation.

What does 1 John 5:14 say about praying anything in God's will?

It is His will for us to live on earth the way it is in heaven, therefore when we pray for His help to live this way, He will help and strengthen us to do His will.

And when we are living within His general will and praying circumstances line up with His will, we know He hears and delights in answering.

Furthermore, when we have a good grasp on His general will, it is easy to discover and follow His specific will. I can't wait to talk with you about that tomorrow.

I pray you "may be filled with the knowledge of his will in all spiritual wisdom and understanding" (Colossians 1:9).

Day Four

YOUR PURPOSE, HIS PLAN

In all your ways acknowledge him, and he will
make straight your paths.

—Proverbs 3:6

We often seek to know God's will for us specifically when it comes to deciding our career, where to live, who to marry, etc., and we do not pay enough attention to His general will, as we talked about yesterday. But when we live according to God's general will, then we are on the right road to discovering His specific will for our lives. This is why when I coach people who are trying to discover God's specific will, I first ask questions about how they are lining up their life with God's general will. Otherwise the search can be futile.

Are there ways you could better line your life up with God's general will in order to better realize God's specific, personal will for your life?

Another important question is, are you spending time in the Word and in prayer regularly? We must abide with God in the Word and prayer until we know Him well enough to know His will—general and specific. As we spend time with Him we begin to be able to discern how each circumstance of our life lines up with His instructions and character. We gain wisdom from His Word, and we recognize the leading of the Holy Spirit through prayer.

However, sometimes factors within ourselves keep us from being confident to know and do what God purposes for us. Doubt, fear, and insecurity can be crippling and can hold us back from our full, God-given potential and purpose. Look at Ephesians 2:10 and answer the following questions.

What are we?

What are we created for?

Why?

We are to walk in the purposes God planned for each of us, not keep them hidden. He has gifted and equipped each one of us. Turn to 1 Corinthians 12:4–11 and answer the following questions.

What is given to each believer?

Who gives them?

Who empowers them?

For what purpose?

Is everyone given the same? (See verses 27–30.)

What are you good at? What are you passionate about? What stirs your soul? (Be sure to see this week's exercise for further study following today's lesson.) Do you have an idea or desire that keeps recurring in your life? These are clues to what you were made for and what God's purpose is for you. God placed that desire, that talent, that dream in you, and He will be with you as you use it to serve Him and others.

Read Ephesians 2:10 again, and rewrite it here, personalizing it for yourself.

When you do what God planned for you, you bring Him glory, not to mention how fulfilled it will make you as you use your gifts to bless others and receive the desires of your heart. But many people never step out in faith; they're "waiting to hear from God" or are afraid to make a wrong move.

What does Psalm 37:5 tell us to do?

What does it say God will do when we commit our way and trust Him?

What does Proverbs 16:9 say happens as we make our plans?

Let's look at an example of trusting God to establish our steps from Scripture. When the Israelites fled Egypt and were encamped by the sea, suddenly they saw the Egyptians pursuing them. They panicked and thought Moses had brought them there to die. Moses reassured them the Lord would fight for them (Exodus 14:1–15). That's great, but take a look at verse 15. What did God say to Moses?

Go forward? But they'll drown!

Notice God asks Moses, "Why do you cry to me?" Moses was still praying when he should have been taking action.

Can this be us sometimes, continuing to pray when it's time to get moving? There is a time to pray and a time to take action and trust the Lord to direct us step by step. (You can't just turn on the car; you've got to put it in drive.)

That's living by faith—obedience, one step at a time. The water did not part for the Israelites until their feet were nearly in it. God wants our obedience _and_ our trust.

Fill in the blanks to complete Proverbs 16:9:

The heart of man _____ his way, but the Lord _____ his steps.

As we prayerfully take each step, we can be confident God will direct us. We can trust Him to guide us and redirect us if and when we make a wrong step.

And what if God tells us to wait? We'll talk about that in Week Six.

Finally Psalm 37:23–24 (NIV) sums it up for us, "The Lord makes firm the steps of the one who delights in him; though he may stumble, he will not fall, for the Lord upholds him with his hand."

God's will is to bless you by blessing others through you. Your fourth week is done. Congratulations and keeping moving!

For Further Study

YOUR SPIRITUAL GIFTS

What are your spiritual gifts? (If you are not sure, there are several helpful spiritual gift analyses on line. I strongly encourage you to do one. It can be fun and enlightening.)

What are you passionate about? What dreams and talents has God placed in you? How might you use them to their full potential? Explain.

If you were to step out and fully live your God-given dream, how would it affect you? How would it affect others?

If you do not step out into God's will and purpose for your life, how will it affect you? Others?

At the end of your life, what mark would you want to have made on others' lives? What are you doing now toward that goal or what steps will you begin to take toward that goal?

Pray for God's wisdom and guidance into what He has gifted you for and called you to do for His kingdom.

Day Five

WEEK IN REVIEW

Delight yourself in the LORD, and he will give you the
desires of your heart.

—Psalm 37:4

Your Kingdom Come

Your Will Be Done

Your Will Be Known

Your Purpose, His Plan

For All Participants:
Contemplate—What might you be struggling to give up and surrender to
God's perfect will and plan?

Consider—What might be the consequences of not yielding to His will?

Commit—What step will you take toward realizing your full potential and fulfilling God's purpose for you for the sake of His kingdom?

For Individuals:
Go back through the week's sessions and reread anything you may have highlighted, and review the ♥ questions.

Session Four Leader Guide for Groups:
Welcome attendees back. Pray to open.

Ask attendees to share what their spiritual gifts are and how they are using or have used them to bless others.

Go over Week Four ♥ questions together, as well as the contemplate-consider-commit questions, if you have time.

Watch Video E and discuss.

Take brief prayer requests and close in prayer.

WEEK FIVE

E

Enjoy His Daily Bread

**Theme: Nothing is more satisfying
than His daily bread.**

Day One

ENJOY HIS DAILY BREAD

Give us this day our daily bread.

—Matthew 6:11

A near-empty refrigerator and an about-to-be-overdrawn checkbook were not the ingredients I needed to make dinner for my family that day. The few dollars I had in my wallet were not going to go far. But I gathered change from my husband's dresser and our coin jar and headed to the store anyway.

This would be one of those shopping trips when I'd have to add up items on a calculator to avoid humiliation at the checkout. The small wad of money I had collected was no match for the lump in my throat.

However, as I exited my car, to my surprise a twenty-dollar bill blew on the pavement straight toward me. I scanned the area to see who may have dropped it, but no one was around.

God had faithfully provided our daily bread.

What stories could you tell about how God provided in tough times? I wish I could hear them. Though many of us have faced financial hardship at one time or another, for the most part our refrigerators and cabinets are stocked full, and we have more than enough daily bread to last for weeks.

Do you worship Him as readily in need as you do in plenty?

Explain what you think Jesus meant by *daily bread.*

♥ Do we even need to pray for daily bread when most of us already have plenty?

Read John 6:31–34. What did the disciples ask of Jesus in verse 34?

♥ What bread do you think the disciples were asking for?

Jesus had just fed five thousand people with miraculous, sustaining bread (vv. 9–11). No doubt the disciples requested their physical needs be met. But Jesus continued in verse 35. What did He say?

♥ What did He mean when He said they would not hunger or thirst? Did He mean our physical needs would always be met, we would always live in prosperity, and we would never be in need? See John 4:14.

The disciples couldn't get their eyes off the physical long enough to see the spiritual. We too often come to Him wanting our prayers answered and our physical needs met when our deepest need is spiritual. He has so much to give, yet we often neglect to ask for the things we need the most. Only He can satisfy the deepest longings of our hearts. He yearns to give us Himself—His daily bread.

Not only could the disciples not get their eyes off the physical, they couldn't get their minds off the temporal. Jesus informed them His water would be like an unending spring plentifully bubbling up. As long as they drank from *His* well, life with Him and all its soul-quenching fruits would be unending, not brief or fleeting.

Fill in the blanks to complete 3 John 2 (NKJV):

Beloved, I pray that you may prosper in all things and be in health, just as your _____.

In other words, there is the assumption our soul is prospering *first*. When our soul prospers, we are fulfilled despite our outward circumstances. But our soul can only prosper by spending time with the Lord in prayer and His Word (abiding).

Names are significant in the Bible. "Bread of life" means "the Bread that gives life." And Jesus came from Bethlehem, which in Hebrew means "Place of Bread." The Place of Bread gave us the Bread of Life.

Later at the Last Supper, Jesus gave bread to His disciples and told them it symbolized His body, which was about to be broken for all who would acknowledge their brokenness, their need for His daily bread, their dependence on the Bread of Life. Then He told them to remember and, "He took bread, and when he had given thanks, he broke it, and gave it to them, saying, 'This is my body, which is given for you. Do this is remembrance of me'" (Luke 22:19).

In referencing Deuteronomy 8:3, what did Jesus explain we do and do not live by in Matthew 4:4?

What does 2 Timothy 3:16 say comes from God's mouth?

According to Genesis 2:7 and Job 33:4, what else came from His mouth, or *breath*?

Explain how you see the connection between these verses.

According to Job 34:14–15, what would happen without His breath?

♥ Summarize what Jesus explained in John 6:32–33 and 49–50 (Jesus was referring to Exodus 16).

Like the disciples, our attention would be better focused on our soul (eternal, spiritual things) and off our stomach (temporary, physical things). Our life came from Him and will be sustained by Him and His Word, not by bread alone.

When God fed the Israelites manna in the desert, He taught them to rely on Him, that they could trust Him to meet their needs. But they continually grumbled against Him and wanted more. Have you ever grumbled against God? Looking back, what spiritual principle could He have been teaching that you may not have seen at the time?

The physical manna in Exodus guarded the Israelites from physical hunger and death. Jesus, the spiritual manna, guards us from spiritual hunger and death.

♥ What does Matthew 5:6 promise?

♥ What did Jesus say was evidence of being a disciple in John 8:31?

True disciples live by the Word of God, which came from the breath of His very mouth. To live by the Word, we must know it. To know our daily bread, we must partake of it regularly.

Just as the Israelites had to gather manna daily, we too must take the time and effort to *gather* our spiritual manna each day. Yesterday's bread is not intended to carry over to today. He feeds us afresh each day of our lives, and we should not presume to live off yesterday's provision.

Fill in the blanks to complete the portion of the Lord's Prayer found in Matthew 6:11:

Give us _____ _____ our daily bread.

Matthew 6:11 says, "Give us *this day*"—not this week or this month—because it is meant for *this day*—one day, each day.

Ever notice how freshly baked bread just isn't as good the next day? Yesterday's manna is the same. Remember, He provides it fresh again the next day, and the next . . . and the next. And we are to gather it fresh each day. (See what happened to yesterday's manna in Exodus 16:20.)

One more important point: Compare Matthew 6:25 and 34 with Philippians 4:6, and summarize the differences here.

Not only are we not to depend on yesterday's provision, we are not to worry about tomorrow's provision. Let's ask ourselves, *what does my level of worry reveal about my level of faith?* Does it reveal the level of faith Paul had when he said, "And my God will supply every need of yours according to his riches in glory in Christ Jesus" (Philippians 4:19)?

God provided manna in my desert that day at the store, and I will be forever grateful. But it was just enough for one day. He kept me on my knees a lot during that time of need, teaching me to trust and rely solely on Him. I learned He is abundantly and completely faithful in all circumstances. I came to know Him as my *Jehovah Jireh*—the Lord Who Provides—as well as *El Roi*—The Lord Who Sees (as in Week Two, Day Four).

We could discuss all kinds of ways to get our prayers answered, but if you're looking for a magic formula, look no further than Matthew 6:33. Seek *Him* first. To seek Him first is to do all the things we've been talking about in this study—pray, worship, confess, forgive, and seek His will and *His* bread.

♥ What does Matthew 6:33 say will happen once we seek Him first? (You may want to look back at verses 31–32.)

> **The meaning of prayer is that we get hold of God, not the answer.**
> —Oswald Chambers,
> *My Utmost for His Highest*

Daily, He provides fresh, spiritually nutritious and satisfying bread for us, just as He provided manna for the Israelites. This world is a wilderness in which we wander until we reach our Promised Land. We cannot make the trip without our daily bread, our daily provision of spiritual manna. Have you been filled with Bread of Life today?

Day Two

ENRICHED BY HIS DAILY BREAD

I am the bread of life; whoever comes to me shall not hunger,
and whoever believes in me shall never thirst.

—John 6:35

There are a lot of foods that the more we have, the more we want, like freshly baked bread or salty or sweet things.

Spiritual things are the same way. You may have noticed when you neglect your time with the Lord, your desire dwindles. But when you maintain consistent time with Him, desire increases. It's like warm, freshly baked bread. It's difficult to stop at one piece.

♥ What do you like to eat that you just can't stop once you start?

Yesterday we learned God longs to give us Himself. He gave us Himself through Jesus, the Bread of Life. One of the ways He feeds us is with the Word, our daily bread. Scripture tells us, "Your words were found, and I ate them, and your words became to me a joy and the delight of my heart" (Jeremiah 15:16).

Deuteronomy 8:3 tells us we live by every *word* that comes from the mouth of God, and John 1:1–3 explains that Jesus *is* the Word. Explain the connection between these two verses. How do they relate to "daily bread"?

John 1:1 states, "In the beginning was the Word, and the Word was with God, and the Word was God." And verse 14 expounds, "The Word became flesh and dwelt among us." Jesus is the Word in the flesh.

In John 6:35, Jesus revealed He is the Bread of Life. When we talk about the Bread of Life, we are talking about the Word of God, Jesus, the Word in the flesh.

Our daily bread is in the Word and the Word is Jesus—the Word made flesh. First Peter 2:2–3 (NKJV) instructs, "As newborn babes, desire the pure milk of the word, that you may grow thereby, if indeed you have tasted that the Lord is gracious."

♥ What does 1 Peter 2:2–3 tell us to do and why? What is the prerequisite?

The word *desire* (*long for* or *crave* in other versions) comes from the Greek word *epipothéo*, meaning to greatly long for, to strain after, to have a yearning love for something. In this case, that yearning is to be for the pure milk of the Word. What do you think Peter means by *pure* in relation to the Word?

Pure comes from the Greek word *adolos*, meaning unadulterated, without deceit or trickery. We can depend on every single Word to be pure and true. No GMOs, pesticides, preservatives, or artificial anything in this bread!

What do you think he means by *milk* of the word?

Then the verse says, "If indeed you have tasted." In other words, we taste, and then we desire more. The only reason we crave a food is because we have first made the decision to taste it.

We taste that the Lord is gracious when we experience Him in the Word as our daily bread. Peter urges us to crave the milk of the Word in order to grow by it. But how do we begin to desire or crave it? The prerequisite is that you have tasted.

Peter compares it to the hunger of a newborn baby. A baby needs milk to survive. So as a baby Christian who has tasted the Word, we desire more of it as we realize we cannot thrive spiritually without it. This helps us grow up in our salvation.

Like our prayer time in Week One, we must proactively make the decision to get into the Word to taste it. Once we have tasted it, we will begin to desire more, as in Peter's example of a newborn baby who craves milk.

> How sweet are your words to my taste, sweeter than honey to my mouth!
>
> —Psalm 119:103

Mark where you rate on the spiritual hunger scale below.

|---|
No Appetite   Craving My Daily Bread

How might you spoil your appetite for God?

Sometimes we don't recognize that food cravings are our body telling us we need something nutritionally. We mistake the craving for being hungry and fill it with the wrong foods and continue to have cravings. It can be the same spiritually. We can have an emptiness inside and try to fill it with worldly things, the junk food of the world, instead of His pure spiritual milk and nutritious bread of the Word. We are hungry for God and His Word, and sometimes we don't even recognize it.

Compare the definition of *epipothéo* mentioned previously and where you marked your spiritual hunger. How satisfied are you with your desire for God and His Word? What do you need to do to further grow in your salvation?

Let's look at another important point. Read Hebrews 5:12–14. What do you think is the difference between the milk and solid food of the Word?

♥ What are some examples of the meat of the Word versus milk?

Read Hebrews 6:1. What is wrong with milk when you should be consuming the meat of the Word?

> We cannot plead ignorance or inability, only disinterest and neglect.
>
> —John MacArthur, *MacArthur New Testament Commentary*

Just as babies don't stop eating once they've grown up, we as Christians don't either. Our food changes, though, to a more complex diet as our digestive system matures. Likewise, our spiritual understanding of the Word grows.

In Hebrews, believers are chastised for continuing to consume the milk of the Word when they should have been on meat, and therefore they had stopped growing. The more we grow, the more we should desire the deeper understanding of God's Word.

Remember, no matter where we are in our spiritual growth, this study is to encourage us to go further. We will never be full-grown Christians this side of heaven.

> We should begin the day with the Bible, and as it comes to a close let the Word speak its wisdom to our souls. Let it be the Staff of Life upon which our spirit is nourished. Let it be the Sword of the Spirit which cuts away the evil of our lives and fashions us in His image and likeness.
>
> —Billy Graham, *Billy Graham in Quotes*

What are you regularly nourished by—milk or meat? Are you growing in your knowledge of the Word? Are you growing in your obedience to Christ? Is the fruit of the Spirit increasing in your life (Galatians 5:22–23)?

Furthermore, what kind of soul food are you regularly feeding on and how much? Under each type of food, write what percentage, out of 100, each type of food takes up in your life.

Candy of the World (Moral Junk Food)	Mostly Processed Food (Watered-Down Gospel)	Bread of Life (Word of God)
_____%	_____%	_____%

How long have you been in the faith? What do you think you need at this point of your spiritual journey? How will you fill that need?

What do we need in order to understand and interpret His Word according to 1 Corinthians 2:12–14?

His Holy Spirit given to us at our spiritual birth gives us new life, transforms us from the inside out, renews our minds, and enables us to understand His Word.

We don't live by what we put in our mouths but what we put in our souls.

Our very lives are from Him and sustained by Him alone. We cannot live spiritually abundant lives apart from Him, the Bread of Life . . . apart from His daily bread, the Word of God, and His Holy Spirit.

> Here I am: I and my Bible. I will not, I dare not, vary from this book, either in great things or in small. I have no power to dispense with one jot or tittle of what is contained therein.
>
> I am determined to be a Bible Christian, not almost, but altogether. Who will meet me on this ground? Join me on this, or not at all.
>
> —John Wesley, "Sermon CXVI: Causes of the Inefficacy of Christianity," *Sermons on Several Occasions*

And he said to me, "Son of man, feed your belly with this scroll that I give you and fill your stomach with it." Then I ate it, and it was in my mouth as sweet as honey.

—Ezekiel 3:3

♥ What would it be like without His Word? (See Matthew 22:29.)

♥ In contrast, the benefits of the Word of God are innumerable. Let's look at the many benefits of the wisdom of the Word mentioned in Proverbs 3. (Note: The wisdom spoken of in Proverbs is believed by many to be Jesus. See Proverbs 8:22, 27–28; 1 Corinthians 1:30; 2:7; Ephesians 1:17; and Colossians 2:3.) List as many as you can find.

Fill in the blanks to complete Proverbs 3:15:

Nothing you _____ can _____ with her.

Truly, nothing compares.

We need physical food daily for our physical life, but we need His spiritual food daily for our spiritual life.

According to John 15:7 what happens when you gather spiritual food each day?

Sounds like some answered prayer to me! (We'll talk more about that tomorrow.)

Back in Week One, we set aside a planned time to pray. Besides this study, how can you include more time for reading your Bible in addition to praying? What Bible study or reading plan will you do next? I encourage you to stay in the meat of the Word so you may experience all the blessings and nourishment it provides.

Day Three

ENDLESSLY ABIDE

If you abide in me, and my words abide in you, ask whatever
you wish, and it will be done for you.

—John 15:7

I live in Florida and have weathered several hurricanes. Boarding up our homes and purchasing enough supplies to last through an extended power outage is a lot of work and expense. We've endured nearly two weeks without power as a result of one hurricane. Thankfully we were safe, hunkered down in the protection of our cement-block home.

As I reflected on the numerous leaves and branches blown down from storms' forces, I noticed the stronger branches, those closer to the trunk, remained intact. I don't want life's storms to shake me loose from the Lord. And they won't if I'm spiritually healthy and strong, which comes from abiding.

It's a lot like the fact that we must *abide* in the safety of our homes or shelters during a hurricane. If we abide in Him when life's storms rage, we'll be able to trust in Him and have His peace and guidance to see us through.

However we should not only abide in Him *during* a storm but *before* the storm. Every day without a storm is preparation time.

Jesus said, "Abide in my word" (John 8:31), and, "If . . . my words abide in you" (John 15:7). Faith comes by hearing and hearing by the Word of God (Romans 10:17). His Word gives us faith, which leads to trust, resulting in peace.

Are you abiding in Him, so closely joined that nothing can shake you loose? If we are to experience the peace that comes from abiding, we must prepare ahead of time by reading His Word and praying.

As we partake of His daily bread, it becomes part of us. It's "You in me, and I in you," as Jesus taught in John 14:20.

First Peter 2:4 begins, "As you come to Him." I learned as I studied this verse that the word *come* (*proserchomenoi*) means not only to arrive at a goal but implies to *stay* rather than to *come and go*.

Remain in me . . . The verse goes on to talk about Christ being the cornerstone and us being stones in the same building. Stones are mortared into a building. They remain. They are permanent. They *abide*.

♥ Again, what does John 15:7 say?

But how do we abide in Him in a world where we're so used to temporary and quick everything? It is claimed the average person's attention span is less than nine seconds (literally that of a goldfish). It's difficult to stick with anything when we're always on to the next, latest greatest thing. Furthermore, our ability to focus and sit still is increasingly being challenged as attention deficit disorder (ADD) and attention-deficit/hyperactivity disorder (ADHD) diagnoses continue to rise, even in adults. It can be very difficult trying to be still long enough to read our Bible and pray. (Be sure to see the addendum for Six Tips for Distracted Prayer.) But we're not meant to be inconsistent; we're meant to *stay* with Him—figuratively speaking, of course. We cannot stay in His Word all day, but His Word can stay in us all day (if we've partaken of it to begin with).

♥ Jesus instructed in John 15:9, _____ in my _____.

John 14:15 challenges, if you _____ me, you will _____ my commandments.

To *keep* is to stay or to continue to hold on to something; to *fulfill* as to be faithful, as in keeping a promise. All the words we've been talking about—*come, remain, continue, abide, keep*—all have the idea of being faithful and steadfast in loving God and living by His ways.

If we stay, remain, abide with Him, what is the promise in John 15:7?

The key words in John 15:7 are *abide, ask,* and *done.* It sounds like some more answered prayer. Is this the effective prayer life you're looking for? (Although sometimes there's a "wait" involved. We'll talk about waiting next week.)

♥ Read 1 John 3:22 and 5:14 and summarize what each verse says.

His will is for us to keep His commandments and abide in Him, and if we love Him, we will. That *is* abiding in Him. That is what pleases Him.

This is why confession is so important when praying. How can we presume to have our prayers answered if we have lagging sin in our life? (Look again at Psalm 66:18.) This would not be His will. It would not be abiding.

♥ Look at John 15:7 one more time, and fill in the blanks to complete the verse.

If you abide _____ me, and my words abide_____you.

The Scripture doesn't say abide *with* me but abide *in* me. This is the idea of an *intimate* relationship. Intimacy with God happens in fervent prayer when we are "fessed up" (fully confessed of our sins) and abiding *in* Him by being *in* His Word and prayer. And of course it assumes His Holy Spirit is living *in* you (Acts 2:38), as we spoke of yesterday and in Week One, Day Two.

This is why James 5:16 tells us, "The prayer of a righteous [confessed/ forgiven] person has great power as it is working." There is power in abiding in Christ.

Look again at John 15:7. What does Jesus state is to abide in us?

What does abiding in His Word have to do with our prayer life?

Remember, the Word is Jesus and Jesus is the Word made flesh. So when we abide in His Word, we abide in Jesus. When we consume His Word, His daily bread, it abides in us ("you in me, and I in you").

> You *keep* him in perfect peace whose mind is *stayed* [fixed, abiding] on you, because he trusts in you.
>
> —Isaiah 26:3 (emphasis added)

♥ Philippians 4:6–7 reminds us we need not be anxious as we trust our requests to His hands and He will give us a peace in our storms that is beyond human understanding; He will "keep" (KJV) our heart and mind in Christ Jesus. Do you see the *abiding* factor in this verse? Explain. Share personal examples, if possible.

We pray (an element of abiding), and He keeps us in Christ. We have an open invitation to His throne to pray, "Give us this day our daily bread," and pour out our hearts to Him. He listens and answers according to His perfect understanding and knowledge of us. He knows our needs (Matthew 6:8) and is abundantly able to meet them (Ephesians 3:20). He gives us Himself, our greatest need.

Come to Him, stay close and abide, and you will be amazed at what He will do—in your heart and through your prayers.

> Abide in my love.
>
> —John 15:9

Day Four

EXPRESS YOUR HEART WITH HIS WORD

I have put my hope in your word.

—Psalm 119:81 NLT

Yesterday I asked what abiding in God's Word has to do with our prayer life. Here is an example from my own experience. One of my sons was addicted to drugs for thirteen long, heartbreaking years. Eventually I had no more words to pray. It seemed I repeated the same things day after day, and I felt as though my words were bouncing around the room and going nowhere (although with God, they never are). And that was *if* I could find any words to pray at all. However, during this time as I abided in His Word, I found Scripture passages that spoke to my heart, and I began using them as prayers for my son. It strengthened my trust and gave me renewed hope.

> If we thus let the words of Christ abide in us they will stir us up to prayer.
>
> —R. A. Torrey, *Power and Peace in Prayer*

This is one reason it's so important to be in the Word and know the Word, so we can use it in prayer.

When we don't know what to pray as we should (Romans 8:26) or we can't find the words, like Asaph in Psalm 77:4 NLT who felt *too distressed even to pray,* we can express our heart using God's Word.

When have you felt too distressed even to pray?

Read Psalm 119:82. Is there something you have been praying for a long time and feel worn out waiting for God to answer?

♥ Have you ever put your hope in God's Word by using it to pray (other than the Lord's Prayer, of course)? If so, journal about your experience, and if you're comfortable, briefly share with your group.

It's difficult to pray something outside of His will when praying His Word. By not praying outside His will, we won't chance wearying the Lord with *our* words (Malachi 2:17) when praying *His* Words. His Word is truth and it is the very heart of God.

♥ What benefits to your situations can result from praying God's Word in the following verses?

Psalm 107:20

Isaiah 55:11

John 6:63

Hebrews 4:12

2 Timothy 2:9*b*

God's Word heals and delivers. It is successful in accomplishing its purpose. It gives life to our situations and pierces our problems. It is not bound but releases God's will. If we can live by every word that comes from the mouth of God (Matthew 4:4), then part of living is praying, so we can pray every word that comes from the mouth of God. They are His words, and when we pray them back to Him, they will be effective to accomplish His purposes. (Be sure to see this week's exercise for further study at the end of this day for more blessings of God's Word.)

> The Son is the radiance of God's glory and the exact representation of his being, sustaining all things by his powerful word. After he had provided purification for sins, he sat down at the right hand of the Majesty in heaven.
>
> —Hebrews 1:3 NIV

In the Parable of the Sower in Luke 8, what is the seed in verse 11?

♥ And what does this seed do in verse 15?

♥ What does this mean, and how does this relate to using God's Word in prayer?

♥ Look closely at John 14:14, "If you ask me anything in my *name*, I will do it," and Revelation 19:13, "The *name* by which he is called is *The Word of God*" (emphasis added). What do you think this could mean regarding using God's Word in prayer?

Could we confidently say when we ask anything in the Word of God, He will do it? (*Caution*: This is not a free ticket to misinterpret God's Word. This is why it is so important to study and know the Word.)

God did far more abundantly than all I could have asked or imagined (Ephesians 3:20) in my son's life. I didn't even realize the magnitude of what I was praying until I saw the fruit later. There are so many Scripture passages I've prayed for all three of my children, but for the sake of time and space, I'll share only a few examples of the verses I prayed for my addicted son and how God specifically and abundantly answered.

Prayer: Psalm 119:59 and 147—"Father, I pray my son would ponder the direction of his life and turn to follow You; that he would cry out for help."
Result: As he thought about his life one morning realizing he had nothing, he asked God for help. A few days later, he was arrested, which led to his healing.

Prayer: Psalm 119:54, 171–172—"I pray Your decrees would be the theme of his songs. Let Your praise flow from his lips; let his tongue sing about Your Word."
Result: He went from playing secular songs on his guitar to worship songs, even leading worship in rehabilitation and later for youth and kids at church.

Prayer: Psalm 119:18, 111, 159—"May he open his heart and mind to Your wonderful Word, that they would be his treasure and his heart's delight and he would love Your commands."
Result: He began reading his Bible—a lot—journaling, and even attended Bible college. He is now a pastor.

Praise God! His Word did not return void when I prayed it for my son. How could anything be more in line with God's will than His own words?

> This is the confidence we have in approaching God: that if we ask anything according to his will, he hears us. And if we know that he hears us—whatever we ask—we know that we have what we asked of him.
>
> —1 John 5:14 NIV

Is there a prayer you've given up on because you didn't see results as quickly as you would have liked? I ask again, as in the first week of this study, "What prayers go unanswered because we do not pray them?" Why not start praying Scripture?

I still pray Psalm 119:15–16 for my adult children, "I pray they will study your commandments and reflect on your ways, that they will delight in your decrees and not forget your Word."

Second Thessalonians 3:5 is an excellent verse when praying for someone's salvation: "Lord, direct [fill in the blanks]'s heart to the love of God and to the steadfastness of Christ." Who in your life can you pray these verses for?

♥ What are some of your favorite verses? How can you turn them into prayers? For whom can you pray them?

Take a moment to look through your Bible, perhaps in the Book of Psalms or verses you've highlighted, and see how they can be turned into prayers for your loved ones. (I like to write the person's name and the date by the verse.)

See how Jesus prayed for His followers as recorded in John 17. What parts of His prayer can you pray for your loved ones?

David had many heartfelt prayers to God in the Book of Psalms. If you have never prayed Scripture, I encourage you now to begin by finding passages in Psalms that speak to your heart, and pray them over your loved ones and situations. Record your findings.

God's daily bread gives and sustains life. What a recipe for effective prayer—God's Word and prayer combined!

> Come and hear, all you who fear God, and I will tell what he has done for my soul. I cried to him with my mouth, and high praise was on my tongue. If I had cherished iniquity in my heart, the Lord would not have listened. But truly God has listened; he has attended to the voice of my prayer. Blessed be God, because he has not rejected my prayer or removed his steadfast love from me!
>
> —Psalm 66:16–20

Great job finishing Week Five. I'm so proud of you for sticking with me this far. Don't forget Day Five and the exercise for further study for this week. And please don't miss the last week. It wraps everything up in the arms of Jesus. I can't wait to study it with you.

For Further Study

EQUIPPED BY THE WORD

Look up the following Scripture passages and describe in your own words how God's Word encourages us to . . .

Endure the fight: Romans 5:2–6; Colossians 1:11

Entrust our situation to Him: Psalm 56:3–4; Proverbs 16:20

Envision what we're waiting for: Mark 11:24; Hebrews 11:1

. . . and enables us to . . .

Exalt God: 2 Chronicles 29:30; Psalm 138:2

Excel faith: John 4:23-24, 41

Exercise listening: 1 Samuel 3:19; Psalm 46:10

Expand wisdom: Proverbs 1:7; 2:6; 10:8; James 1:5

Expel fear: Isaiah 41:10; 1 John 4:18

Experience peace: John 16:33; Philippians 4:6-7

Express gratitude: Philippians 4:6; 1 Thessalonians 5:18

Can you add to this list?

Day Five

WEEK IN REVIEW

How sweet are your words to my taste, sweeter
than honey to my mouth!

—Psalm 119:103

Enjoy His Daily Bread

Enriched By His Daily Bread

Endlessly Abide

Express Your Heart with His Word

For All Participants:

Contemplate: What is something you know a lot about? How did you get to know that topic? How can you get to know your Bible as you do that subject?

Consider: What might "My people are destroyed for lack of knowledge" (Hosea 4:6) mean for you personally? What kind of spiritual food do you need at this point in your spiritual growth?

Commit: What will you do to begin to know your Bible better? How much time and when will you commit to abiding in and studying God's Word? Commit to doing this week's activity for further study, if you haven't already, to help you know the blessings of God's Word.

<u>For Individuals:</u>
Go back through the week's sessions, reread anything you may have highlighted, and review the ♥ questions. If you have not done the activity for further study for this week, consider doing it today.

<u>Session Five Leader Guide for Groups:</u>
Welcome attendees back. Pray to open.

Go over Week Five ♥ questions together, as well as the contemplate-consider-commit questions, if you have time.

Discuss the activity for further study.

Watch Video R2 and discuss.

Ask: What is your main takeaway from this week's study?

Take brief prayer requests and close in prayer.

WEEK SIX

Rest in Him

Theme: When we rest in His kingdom, we will experience His power and see His glory working in our lives.

Day One

REST IN HIS KINGDOM, POWER, AND GLORY

For Yours is the kingdom and the power and the glory forever.

—Matthew 6:13 NKJV

Fervent prayer begins and ends with fervent praise, as we see demonstrated in the Lord's Prayer, which opens with, "Hallowed be Your name," and closes with, "Yours is the kingdom and the power and the glory forever" (Matthew 6:9 and 13 NKJV).

Not all Bible versions include this doxology found in verse 13, and many believe this was not in the original manuscripts (nor does Luke include it in his account of the Lord's Prayer found in Luke 11:2–4). However, it echoes a prayer David prayed in 1 Chronicles 29:11 when the Israelites brought offerings for the building of the Temple:

Therefore David blessed the LORD in the presence of all the assembly. And David said: "Blessed are you, O LORD, the God of Israel our father, forever and ever. Yours, O LORD, is the greatness and the power and the glory and the victory and the majesty, for all that is in the heavens and in the earth is yours. Yours is the kingdom, O LORD, and you are exalted as head above all. Both riches and honor come from you, and you rule over all. In your hand are power and might, and in your hand it is to make great and to give strength to all. And now we thank you, our God, and praise your glorious name.

—1 Chronicles 29:10–13

Circle the words in 1 Chronicles 29:10–13 that are also in the doxology in the Lord's Prayer (Matthew 6:13). Underline the words that allude to His kingdom, power, and glory.

Jesus would have grown up knowing the many Jewish prayers, which ended with similar doxologies. It was so common for doxologies to be said at the end of their prayers it would have been surprising if He did not include one in His teaching about prayer. Therefore we cannot disregard the possibility of its use here, nor the truth of the words about His sovereignty:

> **The word doxology (*doxologia*) comes from the Greek *doxa*, (glory or praise) and *logia* (oral or written expression). A doxology is a short expression of praise to God, often added to the end of hymns and psalms.**

He is King (of kings), and it is His kingdom to which we belong.

He has all power to do as He wills in His kingdom.

All we have just prayed is for His eternal purposes and glory.

♥ How is the doxology in Matthew 6:13 worthy of reciting at the end of the Lord's Prayer?

♥ How does this doxology attest to something more wonderful than all we could ask or think (see Ephesians 3:20; notice the doxology in verse 21)?

The word *doxology* is not found in the Bible, but the idea of it is, and it is certainly scriptural. We've seen one example from the Old Testament (1 Chronicles 29:11). Let's look at a few more from the New Testament. Note the similarities to the doxology in the Lord's Prayer.

Romans 11:36

Jude 24–25

Revelation 7:12

This form of speech seems common when we look, for example, at the way Paul ended his second letter to Timothy, "The Lord will rescue me from every evil deed and bring me safely into his heavenly kingdom. To him be the glory forever and ever. Amen" (2 Timothy 4:18).

Whether Jesus used the doxology at the end of His prayer or not, it is never wrong for us to give praise and blessing to the Lord. When we end the Lord's Prayer this way, we not only pray Scripture, we state He is King of kings and Lord of lords; everything belongs to Him to do as He wills. In a sense we are saying, "Lord, I know You are the only one who can make this happen by Your power and for Your glory. I trust Your will completely."

> It is about the greatness of God, not the significance of man. God made man small and the universe big to say something about himself.
>
> —John Piper,
> *Don't Waste Your Life*

What did Paul say about Abraham's faith in Romans 4:20–21?

Similarly we state we are convinced God is able when we say this doxology. We must ask ourselves: Do I truly believe in the power of prayer? Am I fully convinced God is able to do more abundantly than I ask?

Have you ever tried to accurately describe the wonder of a newborn baby, the beauty of a sunset, or the force of mighty winds or waters? One morning about five o'clock, lightening struck our house just outside our bedroom. It startled me out of a sound sleep with a noise so intense I thought I leaped ten feet off my bed. I have never found a word to describe the volume of the bang that blew out our TV and left burn marks on the side of our house. Some things need to be experienced to accurately comprehend. More so, there isn't a human word that accurately describes God's power and glory or does them justice. I am not fit to even try. He is beyond anything we can grasp.

> But the thunder of his power who can understand?
>
> —Job 26:14

I'll let His Word describe Him. To the best of your finite ability, describe what these verses tell us about God's power and glory. Personalize them— what do they mean to you regarding whatever struggle(s) you are facing?

2 Chronicles 20:6

Psalm 24:8

Jeremiah 32:17

1 Corinthians 4:20

2 Timothy 1:7

Hebrews 1:3

How are we strengthened by this power? (See Ephesians 3:16.)

Oh, the power of His spirit given to us out of the riches of His glory!

> Worthy are you, our Lord and God, to receive glory and honor and power, for you created all things, and by your will they existed and were created.
>
> —Revelation 4:11

Have you ever felt weary, beaten down by life in this fallen world? I have. Many times. Particularly during the writing of this book, one thing after another happened to distract and derail me. I became weary and discouraged. The fact

Power: From the Greek, *dunamis*, which means miraculous power, might, force, energy, ability. It is from this word we get our word *dynamite*.

you are reading this book now is testimony to the truth of the following verses.

What do these verses say about our weakness (or lack of power)?

Psalm 73:26

Isaiah 40:29–31

2 Corinthians 12:9–10

♥ Who receives His strength (Isaiah 40:31)?

We'll talk more about waiting tomorrow (you'll just have to wait). For now the wait in Isaiah 40:31 (*qavah*) means to expect, to hope, to wait eagerly and patiently. It is to trust you will see what you hope for (Hebrews 11:1). We might say Isaiah 40:31 this way: "Those who eagerly expect to see what they hope for will find their fainting strength renewed."

According to Romans 10:17, where do we get the kind of faith that can keep believing and have peace in the midst of pain?

What did Jesus say in Luke 18:1 we must do in order to not "lose heart"?

The Word of God will keep our faith strong, and prayer will keep us from losing heart. It is this kind of reliance on His kingdom, power, and glory that renews our strength, mounts us up like eagles, and enables us to continue to run without weariness. His power will saturate our weakness as we wait eagerly and expectantly in faith for His answers.

This is the same power that raised Jesus from death to life and will raise us to eternal life (Romans 8:11). This same power resurrected my failing marriage years ago. This same power healed my addicted son. This same power provided for my family when we were in need. This same power worked out His purposes in my life. This same power has given me victory over my potential defeat.

According to Job 33:4, what else does his power give us?

None of us would be breathing without Him.

Do you have a situation you think is hopeless? He is in the power business. He specializes in making dark things light and giving life to dead things. The same power that resurrected Jesus will restore your situation as you continue to read His Word, pray and trust, and wait for His perfect answers in His perfect timing. However, to whatever degree we plug into that power will be the amount of power we will likely realize.

It is worth mentioning the popular statement, "God doesn't give us more than we can handle," which is often quoted regarding our troubles. This is a misinterpretation of 1 Corinthians 10:13 about temptation: "No temptation has overtaken you that is not common to man. God is faithful, and he will not let you be tempted beyond your ability, but with the temptation he will also provide the way of escape, that you may be able to endure it." The way of escape is prayer and the Word and the promise that if we resist the devil, he will flee (James 4:7). Furthermore, God does not give us temptation (Week Three, Day Three).

However, when it comes to problems, sometimes we need to get to the end of ourselves before we will rely on His strength. When we begin to fully rely on His power,

> Glory: From the Greek *doxa*, which means honor, renown, brightness, majesty, splendor; the unspoken manifestation of God; His infinite, inherent worth, value. It corresponds to the Old Testament word *kabo*, which denotes weight, or to be heavy in worth.

we realize His strength completely fills our weak areas. In this sense, I think He allows plenty we cannot bear on our own. How would we ever know His power and strength and give Him all the glory if we did not have more troubles than we could handle on our own?

This is not to trivialize our present circumstances. The burden of being beaten down by life can feel like a heaviness, which is why Paul gave the Corinthians his eternal perspective in 2 Corinthians 4:17. What did he say about our earthly troubles, and what does he compare them to?

Now would be a good time to go back to Week Two, Day Four, and look again at the names of God. What do they communicate about His kingdom, power, and glory?

♥ Eternal weight of glory. Let that sink in for a moment, and then record your thoughts.

The first time I ever read 2 Corinthians 4:17, it wowed me. It still does. Our troubles are a blink compared to His kingdom, power, and glory, which are forever and ever!

If we could comprehend a portion of His power and glory, I believe we'd have rest. When we submit to His kingdom, we have the peace we're looking for. It is in the surrender to His sovereign rule that we find rest and will be effective in prayer.

Amen? Oh, that's for Day Four. See you tomorrow. Can't wait!

You're ablaze in beauty! Yes. Yes. Yes.

—Matthew 6:13 *The Message*

Day Two

REST IN THE WAITING

For God alone, O my soul, wait in silence, for my hope is from
him. He only is my rock and my salvation, my fortress;
I shall not be shaken.

—Psalm 62:5–6

A long flight was ahead of us—almost fifteen hours from Los Angeles to Sydney can be grueling (and that's after flying across the country from Miami, making it at least a twenty-four-hour trip). It can feel like forever, so I figured I might as well make the best of it. I looked at it as a vacation from work, phones, laundry, etc., and cozied down with a good book, soothing music, and my favorite snacks.

♥ When was the last time you had fifteen hours to just eat, sleep, and read (and of course pray)?

What do you do while you wait for things?

What do you do while you wait for your prayers to be answered?

The fact is, it was going to be fifteen hours no matter what I did. No amount of anxiety was going to make the plane go any faster or land any sooner (nor would I appreciate the opportunity to discover how well my seat cushion doubles as a flotation device).

Prayers can take years to come to fruition. So how do we bear the wait? What can we do to make the wait less grueling? How can we *rest* in His kingdom, power, and glory while we wait?

The English word *wait* used in Psalm 62:5 is *damam* in the Hebrew, which means to cease, to be still, or to rest. It denotes silence.

♥ David said he waits in silence. What do we cease, be silent, or rest from once we've prayed?

Perhaps we could cease from anxiety, worry, and fear. Maybe David meant he will "not be shaken," as the verse goes on to resolve. David knew God's kingdom, power, and glory; therefore he rested knowing everything was under control.

Another definition for *damam* is to stop, cease, hold peace, to quiet oneself; or to forbear, which is to choose not to do something, to hold oneself back from something you could do (like worry); to be patient.

How are you at forbearing, being patient, and resting?

> When God asks, "How long?" he invites us to place the weight of the wait on him. He does not want us to wait alone, but rather wait on him alone.
>
> —Margaret Feinberg,
> *The Sacred Echo*

Americans don't tend to rest well. While in Sydney I spoke with a couple of Aussies who stated they thought Americans are too uptight. Indeed, there seemed to be a more laid-back feeling in Sydney than in bustling Boston where I'm originally from.

We don't wait well either. Research shows viewers are only willing to wait two seconds for a video to load. Consumers are willing to pay extra for same-day delivery for orders and shorter wait times at Disney. The younger generations are wired to be impatient from birth. Many of us are not wired to think long term anymore. And as we talked about last week, our attention span and ability to be still has waned.

♥ With this enlightened information, how do you think our waiting for prayers to be answered is affected?

Doctors are known to ask patients to gauge their pain threshold on a scale of one to ten. What if we gaged our threshold of wait pain? Let's assess one more area of our prayer life. Let's circle the expression that best describes our level of patience with God during wait times.

Now name it. What emotion or attitude does your expression depict?

What does your impatience and anxiety say about your faith and trust in God?

Waiting times can certainly be emotional times, but we can't always trust our emotions or allow ourselves to be influenced or led by them. The last expression portrays how we can end up exhausted from our resistance to God's perfect plan. But the first one illustrates resting in God's comforting arms while the storms of life rage.

♥ Let's look again at Psalm 62:5–6. According to this verse, what did David know about God in the midst of waiting?

As a result, how would you describe David's countenance (or which expression would you give him)? What was he doing while waiting?

I see David trusting. I see him continuing to pray while he waits (we'll talk more about praying continuously on Day 4). I also see him worshipping. We talked about this in Week Two, Day One and saw it in Philippians 4:6, "Do not be anxious about anything, but in everything by prayer and supplication *with thanksgiving* let your requests be made known to God" (emphasis added). Right there in this often-quoted verse, Paul tells us to worship while we wait.

And it continues in verse 7, "And the peace of God, which surpasses all understanding, will guard your hearts and your minds in Christ Jesus." That's *rest,* or "peace of mind or spirit" as Merriam-Webster puts it.

I wonder how many times we unwittingly skip the thanksgiving part of Philippians 4:6. Yet thanksgiving and worship will keep our hearts and minds in Christ Jesus while we wait—in other words, at peace, at rest, and continuing to trust.

We looked at Isaiah 40:31 yesterday. Let's look at it again. What is the difference between resting and fainting?

In Hebrews 11:1 faith is being sure of what we hope for. To faint is to be worn out, to stop, or lose heart (like the last expression portrayed).

While our anxieties are stilled, our souls are strengthened to actively believe we will see what we pray for.

Read Daniel chapter 10, particularly verses 3 and 9–14. What did Daniel do while waiting for his answer in verse 3 (see also Daniel 9:3)?

Fasting can be different for everyone. Daniel refrained from delicacies, meat, and wine. (To learn more about fasting, plan to take some time this week to complete the exercise for further study.)

According to Daniel 10:2, how long did Daniel wait?

♥ What happened in verses 10–14?

When was Daniel's prayer attended to according to Daniel 9:23?

There is a lot going on in the Book of Daniel we don't have time to discuss. But the truth I want you to see is this: we don't know what is happening on earth or in the heavens to delay our answers regarding unseen spiritual battles (remember Ephesians 6:12?), but help *is* on its way.

These verses show us our prayers *are heard* and answers *are sure.*

Look up Psalm 138:3 in one or all of the versions below, and fill in the blanks:

_____ _____ _____ I pray, you _____ me. (NLT)

_____ I called, you _____ me. (NIV)

In the _____ _____ I cried out, You _____me. (NKJV)

♥ According to this verse, when does God answer our prayers?

♥ What do the translations of Psalm 138:3 mean in regard to having to wait?

> I think Christians fail so often to get answers to their prayers because they do not wait long enough on God.
>
> —E. M. Bounds

Consider our lives as being a giant puzzle. Imagine the pieces scattered. How long do you think it would take to put the puzzle together? Imagine now that God is putting our lives together like a puzzle. Imagine what needs to happen for each circumstance of our lives (people, events, hearts) to fit together.

Sometimes we think God is saying no when He's saying wait. What wait might you have interpreted as no and stopped praying about?

I encourage you to pick up where you left off and continue to worship and pray, as well as fast for a period of time.

When prayer feels like a long, grueling flight, we can make the wait easier by continuing to pray and worship, thanking Him for what He's already done in our lives and what He is yet to do. We can read His Word regularly, sing, or listen to Christian music. We can serve others. We can pray with and for others and ask others to pray for our situation, and we can fast. Waiting and resting is not passive. There is much to do. But there is a rest as well, as we trust in His timing and perfect plan.

If His is the kingdom, power, and glory, then we, like David and Daniel, can rest and trust He has everything under control as we trust in Him.

> Why are you cast down, O my soul, and why are you in turmoil within me? Hope in God; for I shall again praise him, my salvation and my God.
>
> —Psalm 43:5

Day Three

REST TO HEAR HIS VOICE

He makes me lie down . . . He restores my soul.

—Psalm 23:2–3

A recent visit to a wooded area in the country captivated me. As I walked in the shade of towering green trees, I paused. I called to my friend who was now a few steps ahead of me, "Listen."

She stopped, turned to me and inquired, "What? I don't hear anything."

"Exactly," I responded as I continued to savor the moment.

What I heard was stillness. I treasured its silence and peacefulness. It's amazing the noises in our lives we don't notice because we're so used to them—the refrigerator humming, the clock ticking, the dog breathing. Even when we think it's quiet, it's not. Now, strangely, silence was the sweetest sound I had heard in a long time.

Has your life been so noisy you lost your hearing?

The sad truth is, we're too busy to rest long enough to hear God's still, small voice. Our worlds are whirling and our schedules are screaming. "Busy" has replaced "fine" as a response to "How are you?" Busyness has become a status symbol in our society. It is celebrated and boasted about, as though if we're not busy

Noise, the grand dynamism, the audible expression of all that is exultant, ruthless, and virile . . . We will make the whole universe a noise in the end. We have already made great strides in that direction as regards the Earth. The melodies and silences of Heaven will be shouted down in the end.

—C. S. Lewis, *The Screwtape Letters*

we're not productive or significant enough. Although it has been proven people are actually more productive when they take regular breaks.

Because, you know, even waves take a break.

Take a look at Psalm 23:2. Though it may be familiar to you, write it here.

Why do you think the word *makes* is used in this verse?

♥ When has God *made* you rest? How could that place of rest have seemed at first to be an unproductive place but actually turned out to produce something fruitful?

People often ask how to hear God's voice, how to know His leading. There's no real magic to it. It's not complicated, except that we complicate it. I've read several good books on the subject of hearing God's voice, yet none of it will work if we're not still long enough to listen and hear. Like the quiet, stillness of the woods.

No wonder He *makes* us lie down . . .

The green pastures talked about in Psalm 23 represent the Word of God—lush and nutritious for our souls, welcoming and peaceful to look upon and rest in, just as green pastures are for sheep. The green pastures of the Word will speak to us if we'll stop long enough to read it, and the green pastures of rest will allow us to hear God speak in our spirit if we'll rest long enough to listen. Even though it may not have been as noisy in Jesus' day, we still see Him going off by himself to desolate places. It seems even Jesus needed silence and solitude to hear God speak.

It's traditional to close our eyes and fold our hands during prayer. Perhaps we're less distracted with our eyes closed and less apt to be doing things with our hands—like holding our phone—when they are folded. Giving someone our undivided attention is a form of consideration and respect. Sadly,

> The trouble with nearly everybody who prays is that he says "Amen" and runs away before God has a chance to reply. Listening to God is far more important than giving Him our ideas.
>
> —Frank Laubach

today we can't seem to have a conversation with our best friend, let alone God, without responding to our phones. Is it any wonder we can't *hear* Him speak to us?

As mentioned in Day One of this week, Jesus would have known the Jewish prayers from the time He was a young boy. One of the most important Jewish prayers, recited morning and evening, was the *Shema* (*sh'mah*). The *Shema* reminded Jews that God is sovereign and faithful, that they were to love Him, put Him first, and obey His commandments. It also taught children about God. Some say it is comparable to the Lord's Prayer in the New Testament and is a sort of creed or pledge of allegiance to God. The *Shema* was taken from the following Scripture passages:

Hear, O Israel: The LORD our God, the LORD is one. You shall love the LORD your God with all your heart and with all your soul and with all your might. And these words that I command you today shall be on your heart. You shall teach them diligently to your children, and shall talk of them when you sit in your house, and when you walk by the way, and when you lie down, and when you rise. You shall bind them as a sign on your hand, and they shall be as frontlets between your eyes. You shall write them on the doorposts of your house and on your gates.

—Deuteronomy 6:4–9

And if you will indeed obey my commandments that I command you today, to love the LORD your God, and to serve him with all your heart and with all your soul, he will give the rain for your land in its season, the early rain and the later rain, that you may gather in your grain and your wine and your oil. And he will give grass in your fields for your livestock, and you shall eat and be full. Take care lest your heart be deceived, and you turn aside and serve other gods and worship them; then the anger of the LORD will be kindled against you, and he will shut up the heavens, so that there will be no rain, and the land will yield no fruit, and you will perish quickly off the good land that the LORD is giving you. You shall therefore lay up these words of mine in your heart and in your soul, and you shall bind them as a sign on your hand, and they shall be as frontlets between your eyes. You shall teach them to your children, talking of them when you are sitting in your house, and when you are walking by the way, and when you lie down, and when you rise. You shall write them on the doorposts of your house and on your gates, that your days and the days of your children may be multiplied in the land that the LORD swore to your fathers to give them, as long as the heavens are above the earth.

—Deuteronomy 11:13–21

The LORD said to Moses, "Speak to the people of Israel, and tell them to make tassels on the corners of their garments throughout their generations, and to put a cord of blue on the tassel of each corner. And it shall be a tassel for you to look at and remember all the commandments of the LORD, to do them, not to follow after your own heart and your own eyes, which you are inclined to whore after. So you shall remember and do all my commandments, and be holy to your God. I am the LORD your God, who brought you out of the land of Egypt to be your God: I am the LORD your God."

—Numbers 15:37–41

Now go back and look at the *Shema* passages again. Underline the things God told the people to do.

When asked which is the most important commandment, notice Jesus' answer in Mark 12:29–30. Write it here. How does Jesus' answer relate to the *Shema*?

What better way to remember (Week Two) than to pray fervent prayers two to three times a day? Do you think this practice would keep God's commandments in the forefront of your mind? How might such a practice help you hear God speak to you?

Repeating the *Shema* reminded the Jews of God's promises. It stated He was the one true God, and they were to love the Lord with all their heart, soul, and strength. In return, God would take care of them (Deuteronomy 11:13–15).

> **The original Hebrew word for *one* used in Deuteronomy 6:4 is *echad*, which means alone, first, which in context of the verse means God is the only one true God, and the only one worthy of our worship.**

The word *shema* means to hear, to listen closely, to pay attention, and to obey. Interestingly, the words *hear, listen,* and *obey,* though to us may have different meanings, are all translated from this same Hebrew word. To *shema* is not only to hear with our ears but to listen with our hearts and to respond with our actions. Do you *shema*?

Some examples of the use of the word *shema* (hear) are in Psalm 115:6 and Jeremiah 5:21 and the Greek word meaning hear (*akouo*) are in Matthew 13:9 and 15 and James 1:22. Look at these verses and summarize them.

What does James 1:22 say will happen when we do not hear *and* obey?

See Deuteronomy 6:6. "These words" refers to God's instructions as given in the Torah, the words of Moses given in first five books of the Bible. How can you keep "these words" in your heart so you will not be deceived?

How might we be deceived if we do not keep "these words" in our hearts?

The fact is, to hear and keep His Word as we've been talking about, what must we do according to Psalm 46:10?

_____ _____, and know that I am God.

What do you think it means to be still?

Still is translated from the Hebrew word *raphah*, which means simply to relax, to fall limp. Other definitions are to sink or drop, as of wings. Picture a bird gradually floating down and landing on a branch in the woods. It means to cease, to abate, to refrain, or let go.

Is there something in your life you need to cease from, refrain from, or let go of in order to hear God's voice?

If we do not learn to be *still*, we will not hear Him speak, and we will never truly know that He is God. Silence is golden when in solitude the Holy Spirit's still, small voice is heard.

♥ Read 1 Kings 19:11–13. What three powerful elements are in these verses? In what way did Elijah finally hear God's voice?

♥ Where was Elijah according to verse 4?

Do you spend time regularly waiting in silence to hear from God when you pray? How can you take the time necessary to hear from God on the matter for which you are praying?

Perhaps we abandon the practice of listening and waiting to hear His response because we're used to everything being instant, we have too much on our mind, or it takes too long and we just don't have time.

Perhaps we have to wait so long to hear from Him, not because He's taking too long to speak, but because it takes a while for us to quiet our overloaded minds enough to hear Him.

♥ In Isaiah 30, God tells His children they carry out plans that are not His. What does He counsel in verse 15?

Do everything in your power to keep your patient from regular communion with our Enemy, and convince him that being busy in life and ministry is an acceptable excuse not to spend regular time in prayer. If you can, get him to rationalize that because he offers short prayers to the Enemy throughout the day, he doesn't need to have a dedicated and disciplined time of prayer. And if you can get him to the point where he tells people he prayed for them, without actually praying for them, even better.

—Burk Parsons, "Satan's Subtle Art of Destruction," *Desiring God* (blog)

When we don't take the time in quiet to listen, we lack discernment and can miss His prompting to His greater plans. We must be careful not to run ahead of God. When we do, we risk taking things into our own hands to get them done our way and in our timing. Possibly, we give up praying for that thing altogether. At least we can say we prayed about it, right? (At first, anyway.)

Who waits for who in Isaiah 30:18 and why?

Could the Lord be waiting on you for something?

♥ In the last part of Isaiah 30:18, what does it say about those who wait for Him?

Have you been tossed by the waters of life? Are you tired from treading the cares of living? Do you long for rest—physical, emotional, spiritual? Do you long to hear His voice speak to you? You'll never know real rest until you really rest.

I know the Lord often has to wait for me to step out of my whirlwind long enough to listen. We must make time to be still. We must learn to rest, to linger quietly in His presence, to take the time to listen and rely on Him and not ourselves. Could it be that He's been speaking but we haven't been tuned in to listen? His voice is as loud as our readiness to hear.

He is your shepherd, and He wants to restore your soul. Why not take some time today to lie down in His green pastures and drink from the still waters of His Spirit? Go ahead. He's waiting. And if He can wait, everything else can too.

> Call to me and I will answer you, and will tell you great and hidden things that you have not known.
>
> —Jeremiah 33:3

Day Four

Resounding Amen

Forever. Amen.

—Matthew 6:13 NKJV

As I write this final lesson, my mom lays in the bed in the next room about to mark her final day of this life. She is soon to say her last amen. However it will not be an end but rather a continuation of the long-awaited eternity she began when she first believed in Jesus so many years ago. I will miss this stunning woman, but I will be at peace knowing she is with our Heavenly Daddy (*Abba*) as well as my earthly daddy forever.

Amen. It's not an ending any more than my mom's life in Jesus. Amen isn't a closing to our prayers, as though we're signing off at the end of our list. Amen is a resounding, "So be it!"

When we say amen, we agree with what has been spoken in prayer, and we rest in the certainty that our prayers are heard and will be answered in His perfect way and time.

Amen stems from faith. Faith says, "Yes, God, I agree with You." "Yes, let Your kingdom come and Your will be done." "Yes, to Your daily bread." "Yes, to forgiveness and being delivered from evil." "Yes, to Your kingdom, power, and glory, not mine."

Amen says, "You will, Lord," not, "Will You, Lord?"

How faith-filled is your amen?

Amen is to be sure of a truth, like the truth of Jesus and eternity. The word *amen* actually means "truly" and can be used at the beginning or end of what is spoken. It can mean that what is about to be said is truth, or what has been said is truth.

When Jesus began His sentences "truly, truly" or "verily verily," as He did in John 1:51; 6:47; and 10:7, He used the same word, *amén*. He meant that what He was about to say was firm and secure, completely reliable, an absolute truth. Imagine using the word *truly, yes,* or *so be it* instead of *amen* at the end of your prayers.

♥ Let's look at 2 Corinthians 1:19–20. What is revealed in this verse about the source of all truth?

The Apostle Paul was revealing to the Corinthians that every promise God ever made finds its truth—its certainty, its confirmation, its fulfillment—in Jesus Christ, like the promise of both my mom's salvation and my own. Jesus is the consummation of all God's promises, from both the Old and New Testaments. It is only through Him we can pray and say amen.

♥ Furthermore what does Revelation 3:14 say?

John used the word *amen* for Christ. Jesus is the living amen! He who prefaced His statements with *amen* is now disclosed *as* the amen.

We find the same thing in Deuteronomy 7:9 and Isaiah 65:16 referring to the faithful God, the God of the amen (Hebrew, *aman*). God's amen, Jesus, is proof of His love for you and me. It is the certainty of our salvation in Him. His amen makes us secure, for He is faithful to His Word, and all of His promises are yes in Jesus Christ.

Does this bring new meaning to "in Jesus' name, amen"?

Since amen is a declaration of truth and not a closing, as though we are ending our prayer, do you see why 1 Thessalonians 5:17 tells us to pray without ceasing?

Obviously we cannot stay in prayer with our heads bowed and hands folded all day. The words *without ceasing* (*adialeiptós*) mean to be incessant or relentless. The root of the word means thoroughly, without any unnecessary time gap (between prayers). So we could safely say it means to not stop until our prayer is completed, or not give up until it is answered. It is to be consistent and persistent, to be relentless, and to not allow ourselves to be prayer-less. We are to be proactive.

In Week Five, Day Three, we discussed abiding, that we're not meant to be inconsistent, we're meant to *stay* or *remain* in Him. To pray without ceasing is to abide as a prayerful conversation throughout the day, knowing His presence is always with us.

Additionally, we've talked about being in a spiritual battle and the spiritual armor in Ephesians 6. To not pray is to take our armor off and leave ourselves unarmed and vulnerable, and as we said in Week One, Day Two, we allow the enemy to advance against us.

To pray without ceasing is to stay with Him, to stay protected, to not give up, and to not stop praying for a certain thing, even after saying amen.

What did Jesus teach the disciples in Luke 18:1 and why?

"Always to pray." I think that's the same as praying continuously or without ceasing. To lose heart is to grow weary, exhausted, and cease from prayer. Let's look at a time when the disciples found themselves losing heart.

♥ According to Luke 22:45, why were the disciples asleep?

♥ Why do you think the disciples felt this way?

Have you ever felt so sorrowful you were emotionally exhausted? Explain. Did it make you pray more or less?

What did Jesus tell the disciples in Luke 22:46 and why?

> **What would happen if, like the lions, we were dangerous and fully awake?**
>
> —**Lisa Bevere,** *Lioness Arising*

Remember in Week Three, Day Three, we talked about the word *temptation* being a test or trial? Here, Jesus told the disciples to pray so the enemy would not have them, so their faith would stand up to the trials they were about to face, so they would not "lose heart." In other words, keep praying so your trials will not tempt you to get discouraged, quit praying, and fall away into the enemy's schemes.

Think about Peter, for example, whose faith enabled him to walk on water, but when he took his eyes off Jesus, he literally and figuratively fell (Matthew 14:28–31). We lose heart when our eyes are on our circumstances.

Whether we are emotionally exhausted from our circumstances, physically exhausted from a lack of rest, or spiritually exhausted from a lack of prayer and the Word, our faith wanes during those times, and we are more vulnerable to the enemy's schemes. This is another time when we can lack good judgment and discernment. We need to pray more when we are discouraged, not less, not sleep. Maybe if Peter had been praying and not sleeping at the Mount of Olives, he would not have denied Jesus three times in a row (Luke 22:56–62). I think he lost heart, wouldn't you say?

♥ Think back to Day Two's lesson from this week. What kept David and Daniel from losing heart?

Like David and Daniel, Jesus continued in prayer and consequently was strengthened for the trial He was about to face. As a result He was able to face His trials and pass His tests. What if He had lost heart, like Peter? What if He had not done what God had called Him to do in the way God planned for Him to do it?

To pray continually after amen is to keep our eyes on Jesus in our

> Are we going to order our inner worlds, our hearts, so that they will radiate influence into the outer world? Or will we neglect our private worlds and, thus, permit the outer influences to shape us? This is a choice we must make every day of our lives.
>
> —Gordon MacDonald, *Ordering Your Private World*

time of trial. The way we keep our eyes on Him when we are in a trial is to pray without ceasing, without slacking, without giving up, and without losing faith.

Jesus wanted the disciples to pray without ceasing, but they slept instead. I used to wonder why Jesus asked them to pray, because He was going to the Cross no matter what.

Why did Jesus ask them to pray? (See Luke 22:40 and 46.)

I find it interesting Jesus didn't ask them to pray for *Him*, but for their *own* strength.

♥ What happened in Luke 22:43 while Jesus prayed?

Jesus found His own strength through prayer. Perhaps He didn't *need* the disciples' prayers so much as His own prayer time with His Father in order to be strengthened by Him. Perhaps the disciples needed their own prayers at that time too. Perhaps they needed to pray without ceasing (or pray without sleeping, in this case).

When have you lost heart or been sleeping (not praying consistently, not keeping your eyes on Jesus)? What temptations or trials might you fall into in times like these?

Often we wait for inspiration or until we feel like praying. But we're told to pray without ceasing. Let's not allow feelings to drive our obedience. Let's continue to pray after amen.

For amen is not an ending. It is just the beginning—the beginning of what God is about to do as a result of our continued, faithful prayers.

In Closing

Thank you for pursuing effective prayer with me. I hope you've gained a deeper understanding of the importance of prayer and the consequences of a lack of prayer. I pray you are now more motivated and committed to fervent prayer. Can you imagine what we could accomplish through continuous, fervent prayer? Can you foresee the world we're leaving for our kids and grandkids? Can you understand what we miss when we do not pray proactively, fervently, and unceasingly?

Friends, our world has walked away from the true God and His Word. Often when the Word *is* preached, it tickles the ears but does not tackle the soul. For far too long, we haven't taken prayer seriously enough. And now our families are falling apart. Our society is godless. Our country is divided. Our schools are defenseless. Our hearts are empty. Our souls are longing. It appears the enemy is gaining ground. But I believe prayer and the Word of God can change all that. I know it can. I've seen it work in my own little world.

Who am I to admonish you to pray? I'm just a girl. But I'm a girl with a sword—the Word of God—swung by the mighty hand of God. We need an army of sword wielders. Will you take up your weapon? Will you fight in prayer continuously with me? No, really, not just at this moment or for the next week or month after reading this book. Will you commit to fight in prayer fervently and unceasingly from this time forward? Will you wake up each morning and resolve, "I cannot afford to not pray"? Will you put prayer on the top of your to-do list for the rest of your life?

This is how committed we must be in order to defeat our tenacious enemy. I assure you, defeating us is on the top of his list. I assure you, he knows his weapon, and it's sharpened and continuously wielded. And I assure you, he doesn't sleep.

Let's answer this final question:

♥ What if we *don't* pray?

Now to Him who is able to do exceedingly abundantly above all that we ask or think, according to the power that works in us, to Him be glory in the church by Christ Jesus to all generations, forever and ever. Amen.

—Ephesians 3:20–21 NKJV

For Further Study

RENEWED BY FASTING

We see all kinds of fasting throughout Scripture. Scripture does not command fasting, but we see many examples of it. As we humbly sacrifice and focus our attention on God and die to self (Luke 9:23), we will rev up our prayer life, better hear God's voice, and bring on personal revival. It is sure to be a blessing. (Please do fast biblically and wisely and according to your own individual abilities. You may want to consult with a church leader and your doctor.)

> Prayer is the one hand with which we grasp the invisible; fasting is the other with which we let loose and cast away the visible.
>
> —Andrew Murray,
> *With Christ in the School of Prayer*

The following verses give examples of fasting in Scripture. What did each fast from and for, and what were the results?

Moses—Exodus 34:28

Esther—Esther 4:15–17; 5:2; 8:9–11, 16–17

Darius—Daniel 6:18–23

Daniel—Daniel 10:1–3, 11–12, 19

Jesus—Matthew 4:1–11

Paul—Acts 9:1–9, 17–19

Church Elders—Acts 13:1–5

For further insight into fasting, read Isaiah 58, particularly verses 6 through 14. What kind of fast did God admonish in these verses? Make a list of all the sacrifices God called fasting in these verses. What one thing from this list can you do this week?

Day Five

WEEK IN REVIEW

Rest in the LORD, and wait patiently for Him.

—Psalm 37:7 NKJV

Rest in His Kingdom, Power, and Glory

Rest in the Waiting

Rest to Hear His Voice

Resounding Amen

For All Participants:

Contemplate: What about this week's study was the most meaningful to you? What was the most important aspect of the entire study for you? What has motivated you to go deeper in prayer?

Consider: What benefits would a commitment to fervent prayer have for you and those around you? What if you don't pray?

Commit: What will you do differently as a result of this study? How will you keep your resolve and commitment? Are there any days you missed? Make a plan to complete them.

<u>For Individuals</u>:
Go back through the week's sessions. Reread anything you may have highlighted and review the ♥ questions. If you have not done the activity for further study for this week, consider doing it today. If not today, make a plan to do it, as well as anything else you may have missed.

<u>Session Six Leader Guide for Groups</u>:
Welcome attendees back. Pray to open.

Go over Week Six ♥ questions together (Be sure to discuss the last question, "What if we don't pray?") and review the contemplate-consider-commit questions, if you have time.

Ask: What is your main takeaway from this week's study? What impacted you the most about the study overall?

Suggest going back through the study in the week ahead to finish anything you might have missed, including the exercises for further study. (You may want to meet one more time to go over these exercises and/or anything missed, have an extended prayer time, and possibly share a meal together.)

Take prayer requests and close in prayer.

Addendum

SIX TIPS FOR DISTRACTED PRAYER

o you struggle with distractions, mind wandering, or interruptions when you pray? Everyone has so much going on and on their minds, it can be hard to stay focused. Here are some tips to help.

1. Keep a list of people and things you're praying about. I write mine on an index card kept in my Bible, or you may want to keep a notebook. I have all my family members on it as well as others I am praying for regularly listed in categories (marriages, addictions, health, etc.). These can change often, so I write it in pencil or replace the card as necessary. You may not have time to go through the whole list each day, but it's a good guide for when you do, or you may choose to pray for different people on different days.

2. Pray and read Scripture out loud, or you may even want to write down your prayers and Scripture passages. Keeping a prayer journal is great for lifting our spirits as we look back at how God has answered in the past, but it's also a great tool for keeping focused (and to keep from nodding off). And don't forget to include things you're thankful for.

3. Open your Bible and pray Scripture. The Book of Psalms is a great place to start. Check out Psalms 30:6–12; 51:1–12; 91; 139; 145:1–6. Oftentimes reading Scripture prompts prayer.

4. If your mind wanders, pray about whatever it is you find yourself thinking about, and then get back to the rest of your praying. If you're distracted by it, it may need to be prayed about, right?

5. Choose a special place to pray that will have the fewest distractions and interruptions. Make it a place of peace and calm. Decide what time is best and how much time you will commit to.

6. And when you are inclined to say, "I just can't pray today," Jesus gave us the perfect words. Whether we recite the Lord's Prayer or use the elements included in it, everything we could possibly need to pray is in that prayer.

What ideas can you add to this list? Don't let distractions stop you from praying. Our families and our world need our prayers. Some day soon you may wish you had prayed today.

If you enjoyed this book, will you consider sharing the message with others?

Let us know your thoughts at info@newhopepublishers.com. You can also let the author know by visiting or sharing a photo of the cover on our social media pages or leaving a review at a retailer's site. All of it helps us get the message out!

Twitter.com/NewHopeBooks

Facebook.com/NewHopePublishers

Instagram.com/NewHopePublishers

New Hope® Publishers is an imprint of Iron Stream Media, which derives its name from Proverbs 27:17, "As iron sharpens iron, so one person sharpens another."

This sharpening describes the process of discipleship, one to another. With this in mind, Iron Stream Media provides a variety of solutions for churches, missionaries, and nonprofits ranging from in-depth Bible study curriculum and Christian book publishing to custom publishing and consultative services. Through the popular Life Bible Study and Student Life Bible Study brands, ISM provides web-based full-year and short-term Bible study teaching plans as well as printed devotionals, Bibles, and discipleship curriculum.

For more information on ISM and New Hope Publishers, please visit

IronStreamMedia.com

NewHopePublishers.com

Printed in the United States
By Bookmasters